MOMENTS IN TIME

Wherever one goes across the face of the earth, one encounters
men and women whose lives have been touched and transformed by Margaret Flory. This book gives a few inklings of why
it was so.
> —ROBERT MCAFEE BROWN, **Professor Emeritus of Theology
> and Ethics, Pacific School of Religion**

In these stories, Margaret Flory gives us glimpses into her
remarkable life. A woman totally committed to Christ's mission
in a revolutionary world, she envisioned new responses, took
daring initiatives, and found ways to accomplish what seemed
impossible, in and through church and mission structures. And
while doing this, she encouraged hundreds of us, scattered
around the world, to find and pursue our calling, opened doors
of opportunity for us time and time again, and accompanied us
over the years with her friendship.
> —RICHARD SHAULL, **Emeritus Professor of Ecumenics,
> Princeton Theological Seminary**

The delightful stories that make up this book not only illuminate
Margaret Flory's remarkable life, they humanize and make
personal the history of a very important segment of the churches'
life—the developing ecumenical movement. As a friend and
colleague of Margaret for 45 years, I rejoice that she is sharing
the beauty and importance of her life as a lovely golden thread
through the fabric of the world-wide church.
> —CLAIRE RANDALL, **former general secretary, National
> Council of Churches**

Margaret Flory is a one person ecumenical movement! I do not
know of any ... has ... with a vision of
the global a ... ... and ... for the
human fami ... her rich experience and ex ... ... in Moments in
Time.
> —CLIFTON KIRKPATRI...
> **Presbyterian Ch**

Moments in Time is a marvelous window onto the life and spirit of Margaret Flory. It is full of the passion, breadth of vision, sense of humor, openness to the unexpected, and loyalty to friends that have made Margaret Flory's career unique. She cares, and reading these stories, we care with her—and feel an epoch slipping away.

> —Ross Terrill, **former Bi-National Servant and Executive Committee member of the WSCF**

Margaret Flory's life encompassed the world in love, and the whole world is reflected lovingly in these pages.

> —Charles W. Forman, **Professor of Missions Emeritus, Yale University Divinity School**

Remarkable—
> Margaret, the woman,
> her ministry,
> her extraordinary ecumenical linkage
> and her ability to bring it alive for us.

> —Mary E. Pardee, **Chair, Board of Directors, Ecumenical Development Corporation, USA**

Margaret Flory goes about her daily life expecting joyous surprises, anticipating relationships to bring blessings, and seeing wonderful possibilities in small things. Fortunately for us, her life has spanned an exciting time in the ecumenical church. She has met many of its outstanding personalities and set in motion programs that have affected thousands.

> —The Rev. Barbara A. Roche, **Editor of *Horizons***

In these pages Margaret reveals one of her greatest strengths: the ability to make friendships that cross racial and cultural barriers, that involve people in creative action, and that endure. The book breathes life into ecumenical history.

> —The Rev. Donald Black, D.D., **former staff colleague of the author**

MOMENTS IN TIME

One Woman's Ecumenical Journey

Margaret Flory

Friendship Press • New York

Editorial Offices:
475 Riverside Drive, New York, NY 10115

Distribution Offices:
P.O. Box 37844, Cincinnati, OH 45222-0844

Manufactured in the United States of America

99 98 97 96 95   5 4 3 2 1

Library of Congress Cataloging-in-Publication Data

Flory, Margaret.
    Moments in time: one woman's ecumenical journey / Margaret Flory.
        p. cm.
    ISBN 0-377-00298-4 (alk. paper)
    1. Flory, Margaret. 2. Presbyterian Church—United States—
Biography. 3. United Presbyterian Church in the U.S.A.—Biography.
4. Missionaries—United States—Biography. 5. Ecumenists—United
States—Biography. I. Title.
BX9225.F56A3   1995
285'.1'092—dc20
[B]   95-6346
                                                          CIP

For a quartet of faithful friends: Amber Burnham, Martha Kiely, Louise Palm and Barbara Roche, who read a few sketches in the beginning stages and urged me to keep on writing.

Contents

Foreword

"Events never get stale. Commentaries often are stale from the very beginning."

When Margaret Flory decided to write *Moments in Time* she probably had not read this bit of wisdom from the Yiddish storyteller, Isaac Bashivis Singer,* but she intuitively knew the truth of it. She has not written "commentary," not even a biography as such, nor memoirs in the classical understanding of that term. She has written stories—brief ones about people and events that happened to, through, and around her in her eighty-year-old lifetime. The stories build upon one another, and in certain ways inform each other, but basically each is self-contained. Appearing in chronological order, they span Margaret's entire life of ministry.

Born at the beginning of World War I, she became an innovative catalyst in the life of the church during and following World War II. Her ministry was shaped in the postwar period by the ecumenical student movement, the civil rights decade of the 1960s, and the women's movement in the 1970s. On the world scene, she has witnessed the general dissolution of old orders—political, religious and ideological—accompanied by the emerging of new ones up to the present moment.

In this collection of remembered stories, she shares with the reader a period in the history of the church that was so imaginative and so resourceful that today we might very well

* From an interview with Singer by John Lahr, *The New Yorker,* July 11, 1994, p. 75.

find ourselves wanting to recover the spirit of those times as a means of dispelling our contemporary loss of hope. It is as if in these stories of the past we rediscover the spirit that might help us truly shake off old tribal concepts of "we" and "they," and take on new configurations of "us."

The church, with the help of the Holy Spirit, sometimes acts better than it knows. Its prevailing ideologies or theologies are often broken open by the work of the Spirit among those it seeks to save, so that even when the church in America thought it was taking "the gospel" to the rest of the world, it was actually recognizing God's presence already there—in the people and the cultures of every region of the globe. Its task, then, became one of affirming that God-given humanity and trying to make room for it to flourish in the lives of race-bound, region-bound, gender-bound, class-bound cultures of every continent, including our own. Margaret passionately lived out this recognition in her work with the church.

Her career has spanned most of the twentieth century, which many Western Christians hoped would be the "Christian Century." We proclaimed it in our hymns—"Christ to the world we bring," and in our periodicals, one even named *The Christian Century*.

And though we should be grateful now that the world wasn't brought to our very limited perception of what that meant, it is amazing how individuals and communities, informed by the Christian ethos, were energized and propelled to extraordinary extensions of themselves. In the case of Margaret Flory, we see a life continually transformed by her openness to what God might be up to in her lifetime—through her.

Margaret was born in Wauseon, Ohio in 1914 and later went to Ohio University in Athens, receiving both bachelor of arts and master of arts degrees magna cum laude, in 1936 and 1938, respectively. Later she studied at Union Theological Seminary in New York.

While at Ohio University, she became involved in student ministry, working particularly with Presbyterian students in drama and the arts. After a year of teaching at the high school in Bainbridge, Ohio and another year on the faculty of Alabama College for Women in Montevallo, Alabama, Margaret moved in 1940 into a full-time vocation under the various education and mission agencies of the United Presbyterian Church in the USA.

Her work and her influence in ecumenical ministries has been thoroughly documented in a doctoral thesis by Barbara Roche, now editor of the Presbyterian publication, *Horizons*. In this fine work, Barbara sets Margaret's contribution to the total ecumenical movement in a broad, historical context.* However, for this brief introduction, space allows us only to capsule that career in a few paragraphs, and to summarize it by saying that Margaret was to become one of the most influential voices of the twentieth century in ecumenical relations.

From 1940–1980, she was a member of the national staff of the United Presbyterian Church in the USA. Within that broad category and time span, she worked mostly with students and women through the denomination's program for international mission, whether it was structured as the work of the Board of Foreign Missions, the Commission on Ecumenical Mission and Relations, or the People in Mission Unit of the Program Agency. Through such structures as the World Student Christian Federation, the National Council of Churches, and the World Council of Churches, she was always involved in an ecumenical, international approach to mission.

In resume fashion, her vocation goes something like this: From 1940 to 1944, Margaret directed the Westminster Foundation for students in Athens, Ohio. From 1944 to 1951 she was a staff person for the Presbyterian women's program in the

* "Initiating and Sustaining Ecumenical Ministries: A Study of the Ministry of Margaret Flory, 1951-1980," unpublished doctoral thesis by Barbara Anne Roche, presented to the Committee for Advanced Pastoral Studies, San Francisco Theological Seminary, 1983.

eastern area of the United States. In relation to that assignment, she was appointed "missionary-at-large" during 1948, with the specific assignment of traveling, networking, and teaching in Asia for almost a year. From 1951 through 1968, she was staff for the denomination's Student World Relations, and from 1969 through 1972, she directed experimental ministries as a part of an emphasis called "New Dimensions in Mission." From 1973 to 1978, she was an associate for Ecumenical Sharing of Resources and from 1978 through 1980, coordinator of Education for Mission: Involvement in Mission for United Presbyterians. In all of her various assignments, she was continually involved with the younger generation. "I was learning from the young all my life," she explains. She retired from the national staff of the United Presbyterian Church on December 31, 1980.

In the winter of 1981, she was invited to serve as minister in residence at the Pacific School of Religion in Berkeley, California, and then moved back east to become program coordinator of the Gilmor Sloane House at the Stony Point Center in Stony Point, New York, a position she held from 1981 to 1988. She is now living in a center for retired persons called College Walk located next door to Brevard College in Brevard, North Carolina. From that vantage point, she is involved in helping plan the various celebrations for the 1995 centennial year of the World Student Christian Federation.

As she makes clear in her stories, she came into the Presbyterian Church at a time when "to be Presbyterian was to be ecumenical." Even so, Margaret's creative insight often took her way beyond the bounds of her assigned responsibilities. It was in such situations, observed Alice Hageman,* that Margaret became "great at subversion." Hageman, editor of

---

* Alice Hageman was one of the first Frontier Interns—assigned to UNESCO in Paris in 1962. She is currently a Bi-National Servant concerned about Cuban-U.S. relationships. Frontier Internships and Bi-National Servants were both concepts developed by Margaret Flory to involve persons in new experimental ministries.

Sexist Religion and Women in the Church, No More Silence
(Association Press, 1974) dubbed Margaret the "precursor of
the second wave of feminism," a woman who throughout her
life found alternative patterns to the established ways of doing
things. At a time when women were still expected to keep a low
profile and serve on the sidelines, Margaret managed to be on
the cutting edge. She could always find innovative ways of
making the system work in launching new and creative ven-
tures that did not exactly fit any of the prescribed mission
programs of the church.

"An urgent task facing the church," Margaret once wrote,
"is to find people and situations that express the possibility of
breaking out of the limits set by the realities of the past."

She recalls that she would go to the official meetings of
boards and agencies of the church, but, being a woman, usually
did not say much. However, she always took copious notes and
knew the moment the meeting ended what her own response
would be to the concepts she had heard articulated. She had a
talent for knowing what a "new dimension in mission" would
look like if actually played out on the world stage.

As you read her stories, you will see terms like Frontier
Interns, Overseas Scholarship Program, Junior Year Abroad,
Bi-National Servants, Asian Women's Institute, and so on. All
these were Margaret's implementation of changing concepts in
mission she had heard discussed in board rooms or national and
international gatherings. The first time the terms are introduced in her stories, notes will explain briefly what they are,
but all of them basically were ways of working with individuals
and with groups to cross the boundaries of nation, race,
culture, class, gender and age.

Her charge to a local pastor some years ago expresses her
own guiding principle: "Help those to whom you minister
push out the walls of the church in their imagination and
picture themselves on an ecumenical pew that reaches around
the world—people of every race and nationality side by side
who also believe in Christ as the hope of this sad world. Each,

dependent on the other."

She comments today that just sitting on that globe-circling pew is not enough, however. The goal is to interact, to exchange resources, to search together for understanding and fulfillment.

Is her story unique? Yes. Is it the only unique story that could be told about the church of her generation? No, there are countless others that would amaze a contemporary reader regarding the spirit of people in mission of Margaret's generation, but Margaret took the time to recollect in writing her particular memories. Through them we see how one life touched countless others, and how one vocation intersected many others; how a whole network of creative people from around the world began to influence both church and nation in her lifetime.

She has discovered her own formula for writing. She is a storyteller. She concisely describes a time, a place and a happening that makes its impact; yet she is willing to let the unresolved stay unresolved. She reveals her own vulnerability, her capacity to laugh at herself, her human longings and her search for meaning.

My experience in a "first read" of her stories was something like this: I would read along, thinking, "Hmm, interesting little curios, easy reading, often ridiculously funny then surprisingly gripping. So, is this anything to write a book about...?" Then, somewhere along the way I realized I was seeing the universal church in action—crossing continents, penetrating local, national, world politics, entering an arena of decision making that would affect all our futures. I saw the power of one person to make a difference. I saw the power of the church to transform that one person, to call forth energy and influence and joy from her life.

What more can I tell you? Read these stories. You will see what I mean. They are reader-friendly and they have all the characteristics of a good story—and, true to Singer's adage, "they are never boring."

One of Margaret's favorite tributes is the one paid to her when the Margaret Flory Conference Hall was dedicated in her honor at the John Knox International Reformed Center in Geneva in the fall of 1993. An English translation of the French inscription on the dedication panel reads:

> Ecumenism was her passion
> The young her calling
> Her journeys were her home
> And the world her mission field.

Sarah Cunningham

Preface

One question, with many variations, faced me during the 1980s when I was restyling my life for retirement. Mostly, the questions came from those who had been a part of my ministry during the years when I served as Presbyterian staff for Student World Relations. Sometimes it was a gentle reminder: "I hope you're going to take time to write." Sometimes it was a blunt question: "When are you going to write?"

After hearing the question a few times in a variety of circumstances, I finally responded with a question myself: "What is it you want me to write?" And invariably the answer came back, "the stories."

While watching the Olympic Games in Korea in 1988, I was struck by a program entitled "Moments in Time" that highlighted the life and experiences of a number of Olympic stars. By quick association, I applied the phrase to my own life. It was not a new idea. I had often quoted a passage from T. S. Eliot's *The Rock* and had once used it on my Christmas card to refer, as Eliot did, to the definitive moment in time:

A moment in time ... but time was made through that moment:
for without the meaning there is no time, and that moment
of time gave the meaning.

Before the broadcast series on the Olympic Games had ended, I had made a list of "moments" sufficiently exciting in memory to elicit fuller recollection.

For the most part, my "moments in time" occurred during the days of my vocational relationship with the Presbyterian Church. They are the stories that emerged from a lifetime of movement across the world on behalf of a younger generation that was seeking its way in the world. Over a period of thirty-six years, I worked with the Presbyterian structure that was concerned with "the whole mission of the whole church in the whole world," whether it was known as the Board of Foreign Missions, the Commission on Ecumenical Mission and Relations, or the People in Mission Unit of the Program Agency. Even after my retirement I continued to be involved in ecumenical relationships initiated through Presbyterian structures.

The sketches that follow were written out of my memory. Sometimes I would forget the name of a place or the date of a meeting, or confuse a relationship and have to do a bit of research. But for the most part, memory gave wings to my fingers as I typed. And, sometimes, later insights and perceptions have expanded the original moment in time as first recalled.

As I continued my writing, I remembered many persons in the ecumenical movement no longer living who had made important contributions to my life and thought. Sharing memories about them with today's generation became very important to me. Time after time, as a story or an idea found its place on the list, I was greatly blessed by the simple act of reflection that allowed memory to serve as the mirror on which the special time was recreated. William Wordsworth's insistence that "an event recollected in tranquility has an intent it oft' lacks in the present" was proven for me again and again. The stories that follow reflect my process of recollecting, reflecting on, and then recording some special moments from my pilgrim travels.

Acknowledgments

In the final moments of preparing this manuscript, when I was thinking of the people who had worked closely with me on *Moments in Time*, I chanced to open Howard Thurman's book, *With Head and Heart*. I read these words, so applicable to my own situation: "This book spans nearly four generations. It peeks in and out of a lifetime of people and events, yet it is by no means the whole chronicle."

In a flash, a memory returned of a vesper service fifty years ago in Berkeley, California where I was studying Chinese at the University of California. Howard Thurman had come to San Francisco to be the pastor of the new Church of the Fellowship of All Peoples. His remarkable gifts that evening were exhibited in his preaching. Forever after, his prose and poetry have challenged my spirit and I am glad that I have lived long enough to see Howard Thurman Listening Centers established in many colleges and churches across the country.

As I offer a collection of memories that also "peek in and out of a lifetime of people and events," my deep and sincere gratitude is offered

to those who persistently urged me to write,

to those whose lives made the stories possible and who have welcomed me, worked with me, and cared for me in sickness or in health, in one mission after another, and

to those not mentioned in the book but who have been part
of the warp and woof of my ecumenical journey (you know
who you are).

And now some words of gratitude for those whose skills
have helped me share these moments in time. As all who have
worked with me over the years know, it takes special insight
and imagination to decipher either my typing or my handwrit-
ing. In relation to this manuscript, I was very fortunate to have
the gift of two sensitive and skillful people who understood
what I was trying to say and who finally deciphered the
hieroglyphics. Thus, very great thanks are due June Kushino
in New York City and Jan Trapp of Hendersonville, North
Carolina. In New York, I had the sensitive gift of one other,
Fran de Long, who transferred a first rough draft to a computer
disk, making helpful editorial suggestions as she did.

I also want to thank long-time friend Martha Kiely, who
assisted me with titles, and my brother Fred Flory, medical
doctor by profession, but for me, one whose understanding,
counsel and support have undergirded this publishing venture.

Every writer seems to have one person without whom a
book could not be produced. For me, that person was Sarah
Cunningham. From the moment she agreed to serve as editor,
the writing project began to move from fantasy to reality. With
quiet wisdom and editorial skill, she has guided me through
this experience of book writing, which is new territory for me.
From the beginning, she saw the venture as a whole, helping
this "doer" take each step and enjoy being a writer for a time.
In the process of becoming a mentor, she has become a very
dear friend.

THE 1930s

——— ❖ ———

FORMATIVE YEARS

HEARTBREAK MOMENT

My earliest—and perhaps most formative—moment in time, according to memory, may have been my saddest. It was the death of my mother, Laura Grace Flory, who at the age of twenty-five was, like thousands and thousands of others in those days, a casualty of the great flu epidemic of 1919. Because of my mother's serious illness, I had been taken to live with a great aunt who kept a boarding house for the teachers of the schools in Wauseon, Ohio, where we lived.

I remember going back home in the company of my father to say goodbye to my mother—the mother with the wonderful smile—the most important person in my life. When the end came, my great aunt Frazie chose a strange moment to tell me. I had followed her into the basement, and as she stirred the coals in the furnace with a poker, she said to me, "Your mother is gone." This was early December, and my next memory is that of the family together on Christmas Day when my Grandmother Gorsuch cried the whole day over the sudden loss of her eldest daughter.

A third memory, which must have come in the same year, was the burning of an effigy of Kaiser Wilhelm II on Main Street in our little town. Somehow, in my five-year-old child's mind, my mother's death was linked with the war. In later years, I wondered if this might have been the origin of my own horror of war that expressed itself in pacifism as the clouds of war gathered again in the mid-1930s during my college years. I remember participating intensely in failed efforts to keep the ROTC from coming to Ohio University. At that time, opposing war was the mission of my life.

UPHOLDING THE AFFIRMATIVE

One moment during my high-school years emerges in memory sixty-six years later—a moment of sheer terror with clammy hands, knees knocking together, and heart beating a bit faster than usual.

The occasion was a tryout for the varsity debate team of Wauseon High School. I was only a freshman, but my father insisted that I give it a try. At the front of the study hall, prodding me onward, was a marble statue of Abraham Lincoln that my father had won in an oratorical contest during his days at Wauseon High.

My hard work in writing, memorizing and practicing paid off, and I won a place on the varsity debate team. Over the years, my naturally shy nature seemed to disappear in the excitement of debate. The two topics I still remember, from eight years of debate in high school and at the university, were "Resolved: That the Philippine Islands should be independent" and "Resolved: That capital punishment should be abolished." Still, I always felt a moment of terror when I heard the announcement, "Miss Margaret Flory will now uphold the affirmative."

Now I can say a sincere "Thanks, Dad" for forcing me into a situation where I had to think on my feet, but in the fall of

1928 I was an ungrateful child. Perhaps it was serving on an Ohio University state championship team in 1936 that turned the tide toward gratitude.

I still feel that terror five minutes before my name is called in any speaking situation, but on through life I have gone, trying always to uphold the affirmative!

THE LUNCHEON THAT CHANGED MY LIFE

In September 1936, I was on the campus of Ohio University in Athens, preparing to enter graduate school on a teaching fellowship in dramatic art. A young American had arrived in town from Beirut, Lebanon, where she had taught at the Beirut College for Women for three years. Her name was Margaret Shannon and she had just been appointed director of the local Westminster Foundation for student ministry.

I was told later that she took one glimpse of the gym in the basement of the First Presbyterian Church, where most of the Presbyterian college students worshiped, and decided that it could be transformed into a "little theater for religious drama." She asked the student president, Jack Meister, if he had any suggestions for a person to undertake the project.

"It's too bad Margaret Flory isn't interested in the church," he replied. "She could do it."

"Let me meet her," Margaret Shannon responded. And so followed a luncheon at the Hotel Berry where I would meet one of the most remarkable persons ever to be a part of my life.

Our luncheon was followed by a trip of exploration to the basement of the Presbyterian church, where I saw the possibilities in a flash of insight, and hurried to the university to consult my professor of dramatic production, Robert Dawes. He came back with me and announced on site, "A perfect project."

A flurry of activity ensued. Assignments followed the assumptions of the day: young men would build the stage and young women would cut and sew curtains, with faculty friends contributing funds for painting the gym—by this time a theater. The first production, *Eternal Hills* by Elliott Field, was received favorably.

As I worked with the students in rehearsal and talked with them over cheese sandwiches in my apartment, I discovered a faith I did not know I had; and in Margaret Shannon I discovered a dynamic and unique person: A mentor for my life in the church and a good friend for all the years.

In loading scenery, props, and student thespians on a truck for weekend visits to the churches of nearby mining towns, I began to experience the power of drama in communicating the church's mission, which was to have a profound influence on the rest of my life.

THESIS DONE

The completion of my master's thesis in 1938 at Ohio University on "The Oratory of Franklin Delano Roosevelt" was a moment I had worked toward for two years.

The process included a strategy for evaluating President Roosevelt's oratory by developing a standard of rhetorical theory based on the writings and teachings of Aristotle, Quintilian, Cicero and John Quincy Adams.

I read everything that had been written about Franklin Delano Roosevelt by 1938, in preparation for an opening chapter on Roosevelt the man. I analyzed several kinds of speeches, including an inaugural address, a fireside chat, a political address at Madison Square Garden and an occasional address given at the two-hundredth anniversary of the founding of Harvard College. Many of the documents I used came directly from the White House. In analyzing Roosevelt's voice and delivery, I used the aluminum records of the day, which seem very primitive by current standards. Finally, I corresponded with twenty-five speech experts across the country to get their evaluation of Roosevelt's content and style.

On a certain day in May 1938, with six copies of the thesis piled neatly on the back seat of Margaret Shannon's Dodge, named for her twin brother David, we made our way from the typist's home at the outskirts of Athens toward the Office of Graduate Studies on the campus. The relief in the car was overwhelming! For two years I had lived with the oratory of Franklin Roosevelt and for two years Margaret Shannon had lived with me!

With her hand on the horn, she swung the car from one side of the street to the other, hailing whomever she saw! A man with a cane, an old woman with a basket, a child on a tricycle—nothing kept her from shouting the news of the day, "Thesis done! Thesis done!" while I collapsed in laughter on the seat beside her. Fortunately, the street was fairly free of traffic so no lives were endangered.

Ten minutes later, six copies of "The Oratory of Franklin Roosevelt" were delivered to the Ohio University Office of Graduate Studies, but the phrase, "Thesis done!" was to be forever after a part of my vocabulary to declare the conclusion of an overwhelming effort.

To this day, I read everything I come across related to Franklin and Eleanor Roosevelt and continue to rejoice that I was permitted to choose such a lively, relevant theme to pursue, understand and enjoy. I was not familiar with the idea of role models in those days, but if I had been, I would surely have claimed Eleanor Roosevelt as mine. As for President Roosevelt, I read that, at last, a fitting memorial to him is to be erected in the nation's capital. Nothing could please me more.

ALABAMA INTERLUDE

As I now write, I have had a "five-in-one" recollection. Something sent my mind reeling back to several moments during a year of teaching at Alabama College for Women in Montevallo in the academic year 1939–40.

The first was a telephone call during my early days on the campus. "Miss Flory," a female voice said, "I am calling to invite you to a pounding for our new minister and his wife, Tom and Mary Bailey Davis. Please join us . . ." and she continued with the information of time and place. What in the world is a pounding, I thought, but hesitated to inquire. So I accepted, thinking that time would tell.

I did not have long to wait since she called right back to say, "Miss Flory, I forgot to ask you to bring a pound of grits." With utter chagrin I recall my too-quick response, "Oh, I wouldn't take grits to anyone!" Needless to say, the story circulated widely of the new Yankee on campus with a scorn for grits.

In the winter of 1939, *Gone With the Wind* opened in a number of cities in the South, including Birmingham, which was accessible to the campus by car. So on a certain Saturday afternoon, five women faculty members drove in one car to Birmingham to see this marvelous film. On the way home, the friend to my right (I was seated in the middle of the back seat) suddenly spoke with great feeling: "That film made me want to take my umbrella and poke every damn Yankee in the ribs!"

Being from Ohio, and very much a Yankee, I held my breath and then said, also with feeling, "Well, go right ahead!"

The startled look of anguish on my traveling companion's face made me realize that in only a few months I had become a friend. Her penitence was sincere, and all the occupants of the car broke into relieved laughter.

During my year of teaching at the College for Women, I stayed in the home of Professor LeBaron, the director of the Music Department. One day when I came home from class earlier than usual, I was stopped suddenly in my ascent up the stairs by Mrs. LeBaron, who cried out in deep agitation, "No, Miss Flory, please don't go up!"

I paused halfway up the stairs, wondering why I should not go to my own room. Finally, in great embarrassment, she confessed, "Mr. Fox is asleep in your bed."

I almost fell backward down the stairs at the thought of Virgil Fox, the famous organist, being asleep on my bed. But I dutifully left the house and returned to the campus to while away the time until it was safe to go home. Needless to say, his concert and the reception for him that evening had an interest I had not anticipated. I never dreamed on that day that the very next summer I would be living in New York City at Union Seminary's McGiffert Hall, attending Riverside Church and listening to organ recitals by Virgil Fox every Sunday.

Directing the junior class play was a part of my assignment in the speech department of the college. One night in February 1940, someone interrupted our rehearsal, shouting, "It's snowing, it's snowing!"

Suddenly the stage was empty as all my students rushed outside. Having grown up in northern Ohio, where snow came and stayed all winter, I couldn't believe my eyes. The students were reaching for the snowflakes as they fell, rubbing them on their faces. As the snow became heavier, they rolled in it in sheer delight, utterly oblivious to the fact that they were not properly dressed for such a frolic.

By the next morning, the campus and the town were covered with seven inches of snow, the most in those parts in forty years. A holiday was proclaimed and the carpenter shop made little sleds for the faculty to attach to their cars. Around and around the campus went the students, laughing all the way. There were no snow shovels, but no one wanted to remove the precious snow anyway. There was much slipping and falling, to be followed by sneezing and coughing. The snow orgy, as I called it, postponed our rehearsals for a couple of weeks to allow the hoarse voices to recover.

When I began teaching at this college in 1939, I found that in addition to teaching voice and diction and directing the junior and senior class plays, I was also expected to coach a Korean student, Kapsoon Kim, for her senior speech recital. First came the process of choosing selections from Shakespeare, Browning and other poets and playwrights. Then came the endless hours of rehearsal and the invitations to people near and far.

In due time, a beautiful dress arrived from the student's family in Korea. Flowers were sent to adorn the stage, and people arrived from the town and nearby communities to hear this foreign student speak English. As her teacher, I was probably more nervous than she was.

When it was over, there was a swirl of congratulations to both of us as everyone gathered around for the reception planned by some of the faculty wives. Every moment of this episode was an international, intercultural experience for me, especially the day-by-day interaction with Kapsoon.

Later on, she became the professor of speech at Ewha University in Seoul, Korea. I have kept in touch with her throughout the years. In fact, in 1978 I celebrated my sixty-fifth birthday with her at a party in Seoul.

THE 1940s

————— ❖ —————

A TIME OF COMMITMENT

ALLIES OF THE TRUTH

The telegram from Winburn Thomas arrived in Athens, Ohio on Thanksgiving Day 1943, requesting the preparation and staging of a dramatic presentation for the quadrennial meeting of the Student Volunteer Movement (SVM) to be held at the College of Wooster in the week following Christmas. By this time I was director of the Westminster Foundation at Ohio University and Winburn was the general secretary of SVM.

I read the telegram in utter disbelief. How could anyone meet such a schedule? The details of my reply, and the action immediately taken are hazy in my memory after more than fifty years. I only know that my answer was yes; that what would now be called a "docu-drama" was written by December 12; that the casting was done on the 13th; and that the student actors scattered to their homes for Christmas holidays on the 14th. I remember spending every working moment of the Christmas holidays at home in Wauseon working on the details, planning sets and costumes. I remember countless conversations on the phone with cast members.

One of the most important calls of all was made to John Bathgate, a senior at the College of Wooster who lived in Detroit. He agreed to be stage manager.* Our group of thespians, known as the Westminster Players, arrived in Wooster the day after Christmas for around-the-clock rehearsals to prepare for the staging on December 29. I remember that the cast brought me hamburgers for meals I had little time to eat, and that a cot on the stage was my resting place. In sorting papers recently, I found a battered script of *Allies of the Truth*, the drama that told the story in seven scenes of scattered and diverse groups of Christians in the midst of World War II, at work binding up wounds, both physical and mental, and bringing a measure of hope in the midst of tragedy.

The twelve students forming the cast were different when they returned to Athens in attitude and spirit from when they gathered in the first rehearsal five days before. Through worship, study, discussion and conversation, they had been in contact with students from the forty-eight states, and with foreign students and faculty who happened to be spending the war years in the United States. John R. Mott, the founder of the Student Volunteer Movement and the World Student Christian Federation, was in the leadership. They met people who had been involved in the mission of the church all over the world. Some names come to mind: John Mackay, Robert Mackie, Henry P. Van Dusen, Ruth Seabury and Tracy Strong. The students were grateful that their dramatic effort had transformed attitudes in the conference and they wanted to live out their faith in the context of student life at Ohio University.

The opportunity came within a few weeks, with the arrival in Athens of the great bass-baritone, Paul Robeson, who presented a concert at the university. Our *Allies of the Truth* group was incensed that Paul Robeson was denied a room in

---

* Later John became a missionary theologian serving in India and after that, dean of the Missionary Orientation Center at Stony Point, New York.

the town's only hotel. They formed a group to study race relations in Athens.

To be realistic about what they were facing, they prepared a questionnaire to present to every restaurant, bar and barber shop in town. Before long, the *Athens Messenger* and the university paper, the *Green and White*, were involved, publishing editorials and various articles dealing with the issue of discrimination. The students also formed a speakers bureau and offered to appear at any interested organization in the community and on the campus. By spring of that year, practically all of the local businesses had agreed to conform to the law of Ohio, opening restaurants and barber shops to all the people.

Now my story leaps ahead ten years to a committee meeting at a YMCA-YWCA camp in Pauling, New York where an SVM Committee was trying to determine where the next quadrennial conference would be held. When I proposed Ohio University, someone inquired, "But Margaret, can we risk holding this great ecumenical event so close to the Mason-Dixon line?" I remember replying with pride, "That question was settled ten years ago by a group of faithful students with a love for justice, who created a new climate in Athens, Ohio." They had manifested their commitment as *Allies of the Truth*.

CHINA BECKONS

Earlier in the fall of 1943, I had spent a weekend with a friend in Martins Ferry, Ohio. On Sunday we attended a Thankoffering Service at the Presbyterian church. A missionary assigned to China, Elizabeth Turner, was the speaker of the day. If she had not come to dinner at my friend's home, my entire life story might have been different.

In appearance, Betty Turner was somewhat unimpressive, but when she opened her mouth to talk about China, she was mesmerizing. I was immediately excited by her stories of the

Chinese students driven from their colleges by Japanese armies. Along the way west, they held their classes wherever they could and did their algebra in the dust of the road.

My deep interest in her experiences prompted my invitation to speak to the Presbyterian students at Ohio University, who were a part of my student parish. She arrived in a snowstorm, and when the skies cleared she proposed a picnic in the snow! I remember that we had it in her little red car with the top down. During her days with us she kindled in everyone, including me, a deep concern for China and its people.

There was a pied-piper quality about her, and at some time during that visit, which featured Chinese food, eating with chopsticks, and prayers for China's future, she put to me the question: "Why don't you come to China as a missionary to students?" Once the question had been verbalized, it would not go away. She wrote the Board of Foreign Missions in New York, recommending me for service in China. Letters and an application form arrived. I pondered and I prayed, all the time asking myself the question, "Why not China?"

Only the conviction that God was calling me to service among students in war-ravaged China would have enticed me to leave a student ministry at Ohio University in which I was extremely happy. When I eventually told my parents of my plans, my father said, "Couldn't you get a job in this country?" And my stepmother said, "If you hadn't got mixed up with those Presbyterians, this would never have happened."

In May 1944, during the Presbyterian General Assembly in Chicago, I told a large crowd of women why I intended to spend my life in China. Two weeks later, in New York, I was commissioned a missionary to China and attended the Outgoing Missionary Conference, departing soon after for Chinese language study at the University of California at Berkeley.

The Board's plan was for me to fly "over the hump" from Burma to west China to develop a ministry among students at Chung Ju University. But what seemed possible in the spring of 1944 became impossible by fall, and I had to face the fact that, given the escalation of World War II on all fronts, it might be some years before I would set foot in China.

Letters, telegrams and phone calls began flooding to Berkeley from the Presbyterian headquarters at 156 Fifth Avenue, New York City. A telegram from Lida Cleaveland of the Women's Committee read: "Board needs you in eastern area beginning September 5." Gertrude Schultz, director of Women's Work, put it this way, "This letter is just to confirm our telegram, to assure you of a hearty welcome, and to express the earnest hope that you will be able to render this immediate service to the Board before completing your study of Chinese. You really ought to be twins, for this winter at least!"

Out in Berkeley, I struggled against this pressure. "I didn't choose to be a missionary to the east coast of the United States," I said to myself. I loved the floral beauty of California, the stimulating atmosphere of the university and the joy of living among students from all over the world at Berkeley's International House.

But in the end, I decided that God must have some purpose in mind for me that I did not fully understand. And so I went to New York in time for the fall conference of the staff of the Board of Foreign Missions.

My commitment to the peoples of China has never left me. And though I never served a term in China as a missionary, I have made three major journeys to the mainland: in 1948, 1976 and 1982. I have sponsored a number of China-related projects and conferences both here and there and I have rediscovered friends and made new ones from the stream of students now coming to the United States from China.

Yes, China has always beckoned, and in unexpected ways, perhaps I have always responded. But even more fundamental to my life story, I think, is that I was *commissioned* a missionary, and that sense of vocation has never left me: "Here I am, Lord, send me."

THE BOMB—LEST WE FORGET

The day the bomb fell on Hiroshima I was vacationing with Margaret Shannon on a farm in Harwich, Cape Cod. The morning after the story came to us by radio on the evening news, we arose just before sunrise and went to a clearing at the edge of the property to watch the sun come over the eastern horizon. There, we knelt and prayed for the victims in Japan, for our own country, and for the future of the world.

A few hours later, we drove across Cape Cod to a church in East Dennis where Dr. Charles Tudor Leber was preaching. Charlie, as we affectionately called him, was the acknowledged leader of the Presbyterian Board of Foreign Missions whom we duly elected each June as the chairman of our staff council.

He was an eloquent preacher, and the sermon on this day was one of the most powerful I have ever heard—a call to repentance on the part of our country for introducing this horrible power of destruction into the world. We grieved that we must now deal with the horror of the atomic bomb. For the rest of my life I would be reminded to seek a Christian perspective on the events of world politics.

At that time I had never been to Japan, and I knew only one person of Japanese origin. Three years later, I would teach for a spring term at Tokyo Women's Christian College, become thoroughly immersed in Japanese life and culture, and meet a group of students and faculty who have been dear friends through all the years. Some of them had friends and relatives who had perished at Hiroshima.

But this moment in time is about Charlie Leber. Just recently I have come to realize how much I learned from him as I sat under his tutelage at staff meetings for fifteen years until 1959 when he dropped dead of a heart attack in the midst of the Assembly of the World Presbyterian Alliance in Brazil. As I helped prepare the memorial service in which colleagues from all over the world participated, I was made keenly aware of his prophetic leadership in world Christianity.

Thirty some years would go by before I would have an opportunity to remind the Presbyterian and ecumenical family of the remarkably creative contribution of Charles Tudor Leber to the universal church.

In 1992, on a visit to Stony Point Center, the ecumenical mission center some forty miles north of New York City, I stayed in Leber Lodge, named in the late 1940s for Charlie. Now it was filled with nondescript furniture and looking very shabby. Remembering Charlie's style and elegance, I asked Jim and Louise Palm, directors of the center, for permission to launch a redecorating project. With the artistic help of a local committee and the monetary help of those who had cherished Dr. Leber as a colleague, the apartment was transformed into a "prophet's chamber" with beautiful antique furniture and art work, all donated. The four books he had authored, travel letters from abroad, and various other papers were bound in maroon leather and a collection of photographs was framed to stimulate both memory and gratitude. On the day of dedication, October 18, 1992, a commemorative service was held, with Richard Shaull, Robert Lehman, Charles Forman and myself (all missionary colleagues who had served under Charlie's leadership) giving the verbal tributes. In my remarks, I recalled the prophetic challenge of the atomic bomb sermon of 1945.

His children and grandchildren were a part of the gathering. When the service was over someone heard his eldest son, Charles T. Leber, Jr. say, "Dad was ahead of his time and right about a good many things." That was a sentiment his friends and colleagues could certainly echo.

A NEW NAME, A NEW FAMILY

All who attended the National Meeting of United Presbyterian Women in Grand Rapids, Michigan in May 1946 had a particular moment to cherish: The Reverend Tamaki Uemura, the first woman ordained to the Christian ministry in Japan after World War II, clad in a simple gray kimono, climbed the steep stairway into the pulpit of the host church sanctuary and offered a prayer for reconciliation among the peoples and the nations. That moment initiated other valuable moments for many people following the meeting, but I want to tell about my own experience.

A month later, Tamaki, and I as her assigned traveling companion, were on a train en route to Boston. We talked about many things, and suddenly she asked my birth date. When I replied, "May 13," she responded in pleased surprise. "Why, that's the date of my daughter Machiko's birthday." Then, spontaneously but persuasively, she said, "You shall be my American daughter." And I was—for over thirty-five years—until her death in 1982.

In 1948, when I was on an overseas mission to students under our denomination's New Life Movement, she was my pastor and my best friend in Japan. I met her daughter, my Japanese sister, and received a new name—Masuko Hanano—meaning "a pearl hidden in the flower fields." Scheduled to speak at the Christian colleges of Japan, I traveled with Tamaki, then the president of the YWCA of Japan, as my guide and interpreter.

From that time forward, a cable of congratulations came every year on my birthday. Having lost my mother when I was a small girl of five, I felt grateful to God for a new mother from the country of my second love.

A TRUE CHURCH OF THE MASTER

Much reflection preceded my choice of a church home in New York City. In fact, it took me almost three years to make that choice. In the meantime, I was away from New York on many a Sunday, visiting campuses or speaking in churches. When I was in the city, I visited around. I went to churches with well-known preachers and affluent members. I went to churches in the neighborhood where I lived. I also attended a congregation of black Presbyterians whose pastor, Jim Robinson, was a member of our Board of Foreign Missions, and where I had found a remarkably powerful service of communion.

Finally, I summoned up the courage to talk to the pastor about becoming a member. He seemed genuinely pleased, saying that he dreamed of a church where all Christians would feel welcome and would work together in joy, faithfulness and hope.

Soon after, I sat with Dr. Robinson and the members of his session in the Church of the Master at 123rd Street and Morningside Avenue in Harlem, undergoing questioning as a potential parishioner. The year was 1947. My interview was barely under way when Dr. Robinson was called to the telephone, and I was left to face elders who may have wondered why this white woman wanted to seek membership in their church.

As I recall, I told them how impressed I was with their outreach into the community: with the way they had reached out to young people who had run afoul of the law, with how they provided psychological services for those in need, with their summer camp program for city kids, with the founding of the first interracial hospital in New York City (Sydenham, which was just a few blocks away). I mentioned the powerful preaching of Jim Robinson, which stayed with me all week. And then I came to my most important reason for wanting to join the Church of the Master: "Nowhere have I found the amazing quality of worship that I have experienced here in the spirituals and the glorious communion service."

On that note, the elders seemed convinced of my sincerity and they received me with great enthusiasm. Later, I would join them as the first white elder of the Church of the Master. When I made my first trip to Asia the following year, I carried gift Bibles from our church to churches in Japan, Korea, the Philippines and China. I planned an Asian journey for Dr. Robinson, who spoke to thousands of students in ten countries, and I worked to bring foreign students from the schools on the hill—Columbia University and Barnard College—to the Church of the Master for an "International Students' Day." When the students had worshiped with us once, followed by lunch with church members, they frequently returned individually for worship and renewed community.

Over the years, the Church of the Master was a living laboratory for me, providing the kind of lessons I needed for life and work in a world that was gradually being transformed into a global community. By 1972 Jim Robinson had died, but each year a host of students continued to participate in "Crossroads Africa," a summer program that Dr. Robinson had founded in 1960. The churches of the new nations of Africa kept sending their leaders to worship in the church on the corner of 123rd Street and Morningside Avenue in New York City. It was truly a church that helped prepare many of us for living in the 1960s and beyond.

EN ROUTE TO JAPAN

For a good part of my life, I have had the conviction that the Lord speaks to me through cables. It all started when I was invited by cable to teach for the spring quarter at the Tokyo Women's Christian College, Joshi Dai, as a part of a mission to students in East Asia. No sooner had I replied than a second cable arrived, saying, "Bring bed."

My hosts feared that I could not adapt to sleeping on a mat—opened out at night and rolled up during the day. So, the bed and I left the United States on the *General Gordon* in the spring of 1948. The *Gordon* was a converted troop ship and twenty women and children were assigned to one cabin. Because many were seasick and I was not, it behooved me to spend my time on deck, which I did, enjoying every minute of the sound of waves and the feel of blowing mist.

But on the last night, I felt a sudden sharp pain that caused me to writhe in my deck chair and to miss dinner. When the dinner hour was over, Helene Newman, a Presbyterian missionary nurse, came to find me.

"Why didn't you contact the ship's doctor?" she asked when she realized my condition. I replied, "I did not want to bother him," whereupon she went in search. Returning with doctor in tow, and after a knowing exchange of glances between the two, she followed the doctor's orders and gave me something to put me to sleep. I learned later that Helene had stayed up all night checking my temperature and changing ice packs.

When I awakened the next morning, the bands were playing and everyone was excited about spending the day in Honolulu. I had been told to stay in bed until the doctor arrived. When he came, he said, "Miss Flory, I think you're going to need medical attention on shore. Do you have any connections?"

"No!" I replied.

At that moment, a friendly voice rang out, "Oh yes she does. Let me take her in charge."

A woman moved into view and introduced herself to the doctor. "I'm Dot Hacket. My husband, Alan Hacket, is the pastor of the Central Union Church. I'll take Miss Flory to the hospital, and if she does not have to stay, I'll take her home and she can rest in the garden or in our guest room. I'll bring her back in time to sail this evening."

Nothing was said about not returning to the ship, and so I left with only my purse. It turned out that Lucy Langtry, a Congregational missionary on board, had told Mrs. Hacket about my plight, and she immediately came to the cabin to be of service. In the company of Mrs. Hacket, Helene Newman and Lucy Langtry, I arrived at the hospital.

I was flat on my back in a hospital room before I realized what was happening, and as I was trying mentally to cope with

an astounding reality, Mr. Hacket, red-haired, freckle-faced
and as friendly as his wife, arrived at my bedside. He plunged
right in. "I'm Alan Hacket, pastor of the Central Union
Church, and I've come down to be chairman of the Committee
on Arrangements." He turned to Helene Newman and said,
"Your job is chairman of the Committee on Possessions. Please
go back to the ship and pack her things." To Lucy Langtry he
said, "You're chairman of the Committee on Morale. Your job
is to boost her spirits," and then to his wife, he said, "You're
chairman of the Committee on Hospitality. You are going to
take care of her when she gets out of the hospital. Now I will
go and notify the Board."

I was quite astounded to realize that he knew I was
"married to the Board," and in a surprised voice, I gave him the
number for the office of the Presbyterian Board of Foreign
Missions at 156 Fifth Avenue in New York City. I was being
wheeled into the operating room by an orderly when he came
back. Leaning down, he reported, "I got that place called '156,'
and a person by the name of Dorothy Davison (my faithful
secretary) is going to call your family in Ohio and a friend by
the name of Margaret-something. Everyone will be praying for
you during the operation."

And into the operating room I went.

It was one of those operations wherein the application of
anesthesia makes it possible for the patient to hear but not
feel—a spinal, I believe they called it. Shortly, a nurse bent over
me, her voice low and reassuring. "Miss Flory, is it true that
you just got off the *General Gordon* and that you are on your
way to Japan to teach in a college?" I said yes, and because she
was so close and friendly, I told her the story of Mr. Hacket and
his committees. I learned later that I was known as the
"miracle" patient because I had entertained the medical staff
with continuous conversation during my operation and because of what happened in my room the next day.

I was very naive about hospitals, never having set foot in
one before. I had mentioned this to Mrs. Hacket just before the

operation, and she had replied, "Don't worry; these days it's easier. They have you walking the first day and out in five."

So the next morning upon awakening, I thought I would walk to the bathroom. It was pretty painful, and I walked bent over. As I returned to my bed, I caught a glimpse of myself in the mirror—pale and wan. So, still standing, I reached for my makeup bag and put on lipstick. The doctor chose that moment to enter, saying in a startled tone, "Whatever are you doing?"

"Isn't it all right?" I replied. "It's the first day, and I thought it was what was expected."

His answer was, "It's all right, but most people wait until they are told."

The next five days were very exciting. (Mrs. Hacket was right about the timespan.) Telegrams arrived en masse from the mainland, sixteen floral displays crowded the room, and some twenty people came to call, including Kent Longnecker, who had graduated from high school with me in Wauseon, Ohio, and who now lived in Honolulu. All had read about this young American woman who had undergone an appendectomy on her way to Japan. They came bearing books, magazines, flowers and smiles. The hospital ward itself was an orientation for Asia since the beds contained women of the four nationalities I would be visiting: Japanese, Korean, Filipino and Chinese. As their families visited, they looked me over, and I, them.

The day before I left the hospital, Mr. Hacket, during his daily visit, said he had been given a mission by the doctors. "They are exceedingly concerned about what happened to you and suspect that you may not be prepared for it financially. They can't do anything about the hospital bill, which will have to be paid, but they are prepared not to submit a bill for the operation if this will be of help to you."

I was utterly overwhelmed by this kindly concern in a tourist city. The next day I called on the doctors, telling them that of course I wanted to pay for services rendered, but that my heart was overwhelmed with the kindness of people who were now such good friends even though I had not even known I would be stopping in Hawaii. I convalesced with the Hackets for another five days, and then flew to Japan upon orders (via cable, of course) from the board. For some years, on the anniversary of the operation, I received a cable of greetings from the Hackets.

Mr. Howard Hannaford, veteran missionary, met my plane in Tokyo and drove me to the Joshi Dai campus, where I was greeted by Connie Chappel, a middle-aged woman from Toronto who had spent her life teaching English to Japanese girls. "M-i-s-s F-l-o-r-y," she said, drawing out each syllable as if she were speaking a foreign language to me, "there is something I think I ought to tell you. We have SNAKES on this campus." She was so calm and reassuring in her speech that I was not too startled when I saw a snake sunning in the bush outside the window. I answered, "Why, yes, there's one right now." Whereupon she screamed and ran out of the room!

The next day I was taken down to the ship to get my things. The trunks, the typewriter—and the bed—had made the voyage by sea. The captain and the pursers were a bit surprised that I had reached Japan ahead of the *General Gordon*. And I kept thinking, "How lucky can I be, what sheer serendipity!" And though I was to have many unpredictable experiences in the next nine months, I was learning that not only by cables, but also by a marvelous network of friends worldwide, God speaks.

To the Rescue

I met my first English conversation class at Joshi Dai after having been on Japanese soil for only a day. I thought someone would surely show me to the classroom and offer an introduction to a new country, a new institution, and a new class. But no one came by the foreign teacher's residence to offer such help, so I went alone to face my new students.

On the way, students recognizing me as a new arrival bowed, saying, "*Ohio gozymus, Ohio gozymus.*" How did they know I am from Ohio, I wondered, not realizing that they were saying in Japanese, "How do you do?"

Then as I entered a room full of young Japanese women, they rose together and bowed. I smiled, and when they remained standing, I said, "Please sit down." Next I lowered my hands as a signal, to no avail. They remained before me, standing and smiling. Finally, a young woman from the back row slipped forward to the desk and whispered in English, "Flory Sensei (Teacher Flory), you'll have to bow back." And so I bowed and they promptly sat down.

Once I learned the routine, I fully enjoyed bowing my way through Japan. It became a habit that I had to unlearn a few months later when I returned to the United States.

TOKYO BIRTHDAY

A birthday experienced abroad is bound to be special. On May 13, 1948 I was returning to the foreign teachers' residence after teaching a class at Joshi Dai. As I was about to enter the house, I saw a black limousine approaching. There was no street, and much to my surprise, the car was moving along the walkway.

As it stopped, a charming woman emerged with an armful of flowers. She said, "I am looking for Miss Margaret Flory." When I said, "I am Margaret Flory," she thrust the flowers into my arms and cried out joyfully, "Happy Birthday from Josefa Ilano in Manila."

By this time, the woman's husband was out of the car, and he introduced himself as the personal envoy from the Philippines to the Japanese government. (Official diplomatic relations had not yet been reestablished after World War II.)

I invited them into the residence, which had been named Reischauer House for the founder and executive secretary of the college, whose son Edwin later became the U.S. ambassador to Japan. I then called for the housekeeper, Fusaka-san,* asking her to prepare tea for two guests. I learned that my dear friend in the Philippines, Dr. Josefa Ilano, was also their dear friend and that she had cabled them to order flowers for my birthday. They had decided to deliver them personally.

We were still exchanging introductory pleasantries when the doorbell rang. It was Tamaki Uemura, who had also come to celebrate my birthday. The Filipino guests, whose names are no longer in my memory, were startled indeed to know that Mrs. Uemura and Dr. Ilano were close friends. Both had arrived in the United States two years earlier in the spring of 1946 to participate in a team of reconciliation. Three Asian women: a doctor from the Philippines, a pastor from Japan and a teacher from China (Hsiang Foh Mei) had been invited by Presbyterian women to attend a national meeting and to travel as a team to a variety of regional meetings in the summer of 1946. I had been the organizer of their travel, the recorder of all their joys and the receiver of all complaints.

I had been with Tamaki and Josefa when they first met at Wilson College in Chambersburg, Pennsylvania, and had knelt with them in a college dormitory, asking God to forgive past hatreds, personal and national, and to bind them into a team of reconciliation for the journey across America. Now around a small table in the foreign teachers' residence in Tokyo, I was hearing that story told to two Filipinos, no longer strangers, who were sharing tea and cakes with Tamaki and me.

From conversation about the comic aspects of travel in America, we moved to wartime memories, and the Filipinos spoke not of the cruelties of the Japanese military but of occasions when Japanese Christians had identified themselves in relationships that would forever be treasured and passed on to generation after generation.

---

* *San* is a term of endearment or friendship, usually indicating warm affection.

Before my Asian journey of 1948 ended, I was to see Dr. Ilano in her own country. But in the meantime, she had given me a unique and happy birthday as an act of generosity, imagination and love that conquered distance and brought strangers together in new friendships.

BEHOLD TOYOHIKO KAGAWA

On a spring day in Tokyo in 1948, Makino-san approached her teacher at Joshi Dai with a shy smile. "Flory Sensei," she said, "I would like to take you to meet my pastor, and I have learned that he will be at home to receive us next Saturday afternoon. Will you go with me?" I answered yes, without realizing that the pastor in question was the famous Japanese poet and writer, Dr. Toyohiko Kagawa.

When I learned this fact, I was ecstatic, for Dr. Kagawa had long been a hero to young Christians of my generation. He had moved to the slums of Kobe to live among the poor and outcast. We knew the price he had paid in contracting tuberculosis and trachoma. We knew how he had shared his vision and his convictions in tireless travel around the world. Many of us had memorized favorite poems. We knew of his struggle for justice among the marginalized in his own nation.

And I was to see him before the week was out!

On Saturday afternoon, we took the train to a modest home in a suburb of Tokyo. In the early stages of the conversation, I tried to tell Dr. Kagawa how much he had meant to the young Americans of my generation. He listened and smiled. I told him that I had a favorite book and a favorite poem. I told him about my days as a counselor at the Presbyterian church in Athens where I worked with students at Ohio University. I mentioned that each year during Lent we studied his novel on the life of Christ, *Behold the Man*, and I tried to describe the impact of this book on the lives of students I had known.

When it was his turn to speak, he told me of the hopes he had for the "new Japan." He mentioned the new outbreak in Japan of organizations devoted to peacemaking so that the children and the grandchildren would never experience the overwhelming tragedy of war.

After a good round of conversation, he summoned Mrs. Kagawa to bring in the tea as he disappeared into his study. Mrs. Kagawa made conversation in a marvelous way. She said, "I sometimes feel that you Americans spoil my husband." Then, looking me straight in the eye, she said, "Miss Flory, my husband, Dr. Kagawa, is a very great man, but he is not a saint."

Luckily for me, Dr. Kagawa chose the next moment to return to the room bearing a book. It turned out to be *Behold the Man*, the very book I had cherished so much but had left behind in the library of the Westminster Foundation in Athens. He signed his name on the flyleaf and handed it to me with a low bow. To this day, whenever I dust that book on my shelf, I experience a surge of joyful remembrance and a silent reminder of these excerpts from a favorite poem, "Discovery":

> A wonderful thought
> In the dawn was given
>
> .   .   .   .   .   .
>
> And the thought
> Was this:
> That a secret plan
> Is hid in my hand;
> That my hand is big,
> Big,
> Because of this plan.
>
> That God,
> Who dwells in my hand
> Knows this secret plan
> Of the things He will do for the world
> Using my hand.*

* Toyohiko Kagawa, *Songs from the Slums* (Nashville: Cokesbury Press, 1935), 66–67.

There is a sequel to this story. A year later I was on the stage of the Silver Bay (New York) conference grounds waiting for the speaker to arrive to address the Friendship Press ecumenical mission study theme, "Japan"—a theme that took on added interest and poignancy in the postwar years. But, alas, the appointed time had come and gone with no speaker in sight. We knew that Dr. Kagawa's plane was landing in a nearby city and that he was completing the journey by car.

Not being a songleader, I called someone to the platform who was. The singing went on and on. Finally there was a disturbance at a side door, and Dr. Kagawa made his entrance onto the platform. Halfway across the stage he recognized me, stretched forth both hands and advanced toward me, bowing and smiling, bowing and smiling! In return, I responded in the same way, moving toward him, I smiled and I bowed very low. We were making "theater." The audience loved it, and they cheered.

THE STORY OF A CHARM CASE

Kyoko Matsubara was one of the Japanese students of Joshi Dai who came to say goodbye when I left the college in July of 1948. Wrapped in the customary furoshki (a square of cloth with the four corners tied together to form a carrying bag) was a farewell gift housed in a small, square wooden box with a glass lid. In the attached note she had written:

Dear Flory Sensei,

In this small box is a charm case which my parents purchased for me when I was born. Many charms were placed inside to keep me from harm. Now that I have found Jesus Christ, I do not need this charm case any longer, and I want to give it to you who helped me to find Him. My grandfather suggested that I leave one charm inside to keep you from harm. He said, "Yes, Flory Sensei has Jesus Christ, but perhaps this little charm will also help to keep her from harm." I decided to bow to my grandfather's judgment. I hope that you will understand.

Yours gratefully,
Kyoko Matsubara

Kyoko Matsubara (now Mrs. Sadao Kohri) has kept in touch with "Flory Sensei" for forty-six years through letters and visits. She organized a journey to the United States in the mid-1980s of sixteen Japanese women who had been in my classes at Joshi Dai in 1948. It was the thirty-fifth anniversary of a unique international friendship between an American teacher and her Japanese students.

In the meantime, she had lived in the United States with her family for several years, participating in the life of Church Women United. Once she brought her grown daughters to see me. I took the charm case from its place on my ecumenical wall and showed them the letter their mother had written as a young student many years before.

The little red charm case still has a place in the apartment where I now live in Brevard, North Carolina, and it will always have a place in my heart.

THE BLESSING OF THE BEACH SWEEPERS

After finishing my teaching at Joshi Dai in the summer of 1948, I embarked on several weeks of travel beyond Tokyo accompanied by Tamaki Uemura as mentor and interpreter as well as adopted mother. I had a touch of homesickness as the date of July 15 approached, the day of my brother Fred's wedding in Toledo, Ohio. I had intended to be present for the wedding until a last-minute invitation to teach moved my departure forward by three months.

On the evening before the wedding, Tamaki surprised me by saying, "This is a perfect place to celebrate your brother's wedding tomorrow, for this is where the old man and woman who are the symbols of married happiness sweep the beach every night at midnight."

The next morning, as the wedding was about to begin on the other side of the world, Mrs. Uemura called me to the balcony of the room where we were staying in an inn in the Kansai area of Japan. With my eyes on the sea's far horizon, I heard the wedding service read solemnly by my dear friend, who then prayed for Helen and Fred and their future happiness.

Some thirty years later, I chanced to be in the Kansai area as the guest of Teruko Ohashi Sugimoto, now a leading medical social worker in Japan. (Earlier, she had been my student in Japan and later studied in the United States on a Presbyterian scholarship). As we drove in the neighborhood, I saw a sign and realized that we were very near the beach where I had celebrated my brother's wedding. I related to Teruko the story of the old couple who walked the beach at midnight, and she told me that I might be able to find a figure in porcelain to commemorate the legend. We looked without success in a number of shops.

The scene now shifts to the Gilmor Sloane House at Stony Point, New York. Sixteen women in their fifties had come to celebrate with me the thirty-fifth anniversary of our student-teacher relationship. After a wondrous evening celebration, a number of gifts appeared wrapped in the Japanese furoshki style.

"It is something you wanted," said Teruko as I fumbled with the wrapping—a comment that startled me, since I had learned very early not to admire anything for fear it would become mine under embarrassing circumstances. In the box that night, I found two beautiful figurines, exquisitely formed—the old man and woman who traditionally sweep the beach at midnight as a symbol of married happiness. The old couple now resides on a shelf in the home of Fred and Helen Flory in Columbus, Ohio.

UNDERSTANDING PREJUDICE

During a month's residence at Silliman University in the Philippines in 1948, I was asked to meet with the World Friendship Group of Silliman High School students.

Before I could share what was on my mind, a student rose and referred to stories of recent lynchings in the United States and asked what I had to say about the prejudice and hatred reflected in these actions.

As this was going on, the youth advisor was squirming in her seat. Obviously she did not want the American guest to be embarrassed. When I spoke, I admitted the tragedy of the situation and remarked that it was even more serious than they could understand. I also mentioned several groups that were working together in the struggle to fight racist attitudes and practices in the United States.

But then I proceeded to point out that during my journey through Asia (I was then in the fifth month of that journey), I had encountered prejudice that I had not anticipated. I told of the prejudice against the Eta people in Japan that I had witnessed. I described the bitterness of feelings in Korea against the Japanese, and then I mentioned that since I had been in the Philippines, I was quite surprised at the way Filipinos felt about the Chinese in their midst.

At that moment, the quiet in the room was intense. Then, out of the silence, a young woman cried out. "She's right, kids, you know she is right. We do behave badly toward the Chinese. We're jealous because they work hard and get ahead. Instead of turning against them, we should work a little harder ourselves."

Quite a few heads were nodding as she sat down. The intensity of the incident had cleared the air, and we proceeded with a meaningful discussion of Asian participation in the international community.

This experience at the beginning of my international ministry helped me to understand the importance of seeing one's own country through the eyes of others while at the same time helping persons from other countries face the lurking prejudice in their own hearts and minds.

WHATEVER GOD EXPECTS

The plane stood on the tarmac of the Manila airport bound for Shanghai as the typhoon pounded its wings. It was the middle of a dark night in early September 1948. There was action in the cockpit! "Surely we are not taking off in such a storm," I thought. But, indeed we were! As the plane soared into the clouds, space opened, and miraculously we flew into a beautiful Kiplingesque dawn. Now I understood fully the lines, "the dawn comes up like thunder out of China 'cross the bay."

There was a deep surge of expectancy in my heart as the plane swooped down into Shanghai, where a company of missionaries was waiting for me. It was four years later than I had originally planned to arrive in China, and it was a much different kind of mission. Instead of staying in one Christian college for the rest of my life, I would be visiting most of the church-related colleges in China as well as the government universities where Student Christian Fellowships had been formed.

It took only a few hours in Shanghai and a few exciting conversations for me to realize how different China was from what I had previously imagined. The Japanese war was over, but now Communist armies were poised a few hours north of Peking (now called Beijing). The so called new currency was deteriorating every day, and refugees were already moving south. China was in a state of upheaval and only a few of the friends, old and new, with whom I conversed, thought I would complete the extensive travel itinerary that had been planned for me. The travel agencies didn't think so either, but after standing in line every day for seven days I was rewarded with an itinerary and tickets, some for long train rides through the countryside and some for army transport plane rides, with baggage in the middle of the plane and pigs and vegetables in crates at the feet of passengers strapped into seats around the edge.

The campuses in those days were peaceful but the students' hearts and minds were not. They felt they were facing the greatest dilemma that any student generation had ever faced. They had lost faith in their government under Chiang Kai-shek, but they were also fearful of what communism might bring. Some, however, influenced by Marxist study groups, were hopeful.

"What was my mission at such a time?" I pondered. Fortunately I was carrying a secret weapon in my suitcase, which today we would call a conversation piece. It was a small Japanese doll with the flags of Japan's former enemy countries in its tiny hands —flags of the USA, Korea, the Philippines and China. Beside the doll, in a furoshki (a piece of silk knotted in four corners that became a carrying bag), was a small brocaded book. My Japanese student friends from Joshi Dai in Tokyo had said, "Here are some little messengers of peace. Please take them in the name of Christ to Korea, the Philippines, China and the USA, and tell the students you meet of our sorrow for the past and the hope we have in Christ.

The booklet was addressed "to all the students in the world who are our friends in Christ." On the second page of the book was the beautiful chapel at Joshi Dai, designed by Frank Lloyd Wright, with its graceful spire pointing skyward. Below the picture was the scripture from which the college motto is taken. "Whatever things are true." On each of six pages there was a picture of a particular student and her special message.

I marveled at the painstaking effort that had gone into the making of this book and how the students must have struggled over the English to get it so perfect. This was a group of students to whom the Christian faith was very real and who were dreaming of the day when their country could once again take its place in the family of nations. By the time I reached

China I knew the power of the book and the doll to change attitudes and to transform enmity into longings for peaceful contact and understanding. Students in the Philippines were already writing letters seeking reconciliation to students in Japan whose addresses I had supplied. At one school in Manila, a young man with tears flowing freely came forward after a chapel service to say, "My father and my brother were killed by the Japanese, but I am surrendering my hatred right now." Then, pressing my hand, he muttered a choked, "Thank you," and "God bless," and disappeared around a corner of the building, disturbed by his visible emotion.

The story was the same in China. When the book and the doll told their story, the students of a middle school in Nanking made seven hundred bookmarks to send to Japan. The closing words of a letter prepared by students of Hangchow University were unforgettable, "Here we remain your loving brothers and sisters, and we will give to or receive from you whatever God expects." "Whatever God expects" are words of power when applied to human attitudes.

DESTINATION NANKING

It had been a wonderful week in Hangchow that fall of 1948 during my first trip to China. I had been received by the students and faculty of Hangchow Christian College and the Student Christian Fellowship of a nearby government university. Hangchow had captured my heart with its beautiful West Lake and its flowering trees. And now, at the train station, I had said goodbye to a band of Chinese students and to Donald Irwin, the U.S. missionary student worker.

The big iron gates of the train yard had swung shut, and the train with all passengers in place was ready to move. It was only when the passenger agent appeared in my car and began approaching my seat that I realized a terrible omission. I had forgotten to go for the stamp I needed in my passport for travel to Nanking. It was not something to be accomplished at the station at the last minute, but rather, like a visa, to be secured during the week prior to departure. My friends, I deduced, had probably left by then, and I was panic-stricken. So there I sat, sans visa and sans permission to travel to my next destination.

I did not understand the agent's question in Chinese, so I smiled and said slowly and clearly in English, "I am going to Nanking." He took my passport, looked through it three times and gave it back with a quizzical expression on his face. He left the car only to return a few minutes later with a second official.

We went through the same procedure. I surrendered my passport, saying again, "I am going to Nanking." There followed the same flip through the pages and the return of my passport, which satisfied no one. The officials departed and the train finally started to move. At last, I thought, I'm on my way! But the passenger agent returned yet again, this time with someone who looked even more official. We went through the same procedure, but with one difference: this time the official took from his pocket a small device and stamped my passport.

When the two officials disappeared, I sat there feeling relieved but a bit shaken, wondering, "Why did the Board send three men with Margaret Shannon when she traveled to China, and no one with me?"

A GLIMPSE OF DR. T. C. CHAO

"All real living is meeting," according to Israeli philosopher Martin Buber. Looking back, I realize I never felt this more meaningfully than in 1948 in Peking, China, when an interview was arranged for me with Dr. T. C. Chao.

Dr. Chao, an eminent Chinese theologian and the president of the theological college at Yenching University, had just returned from the first General Assembly of the World Council of Churches in Amsterdam, where he had been elected to the presidium of the Council, representing Asia.

As Dr. Chao received me in his office wearing a long blue gown, fulfilling completely the image of a Chinese scholar, my mind flashed back to the day just a few weeks earlier when the World Assembly opened in Amsterdam. On that day, I was on the campus of Silliman University in the Philippines on my mission to Asian students. As I prepared for the day, I thought I might be the only person in Dumaguete to be aware of this momentous event taking place in the Netherlands. In my morning prayers, I remembered the delegates from my own church and prayed for all the delegates. But when I crossed the campus later, I was astonished and delighted to see several students carrying sandwich boards with such captions as "World Council of Churches opening in Amsterdam: Pray for our Philippine delegates."

Now in China I was meeting the new Asian president of the Council. He had just written his Amsterdam Assembly report, and it had already been translated into English. After we had talked about the Chinese Christian universities and their students, he asked me if I would be willing to review the translation and check the English. For me this was a blessed privilege. But more importantly, this was an opportunity to learn what he was saying to the Chinese Christian community about the meaning of the new ecumenical developments worldwide.

I carried that image of Dr. T. C. Chao into the years that followed when all diplomatic relationships between the United States and China had been cut off and there was only silence between the churches in China and those in the United States.

When I returned to China in 1976 as a member of a special visiting delegation, I asked to see Dr. Chao while I was in Beijing. At the end of my week's visit, I was told that he had not been found. Later I learned that he was among the elderly persons moved from the city at the time of the great earthquake, which had occurred two months before my visit.

Dr. Chao died in 1979, just when churches in China began to be reopened. Coincidentally, the title of one of his most famous hymns, "Rise to Greet the Dawn," expressed not only the faith by which he lived and died, but the mood of the church of China at that promising time.

THE 1950s

————— ❖ —————

THE WORLD EXPANDS

WHERE IS THE JEEP?

Could there ever be a moment more frustrating than that of arriving at a campus to direct a play only to find the auditorium locked and the custodian unavailable? Such an experience happened to me in December 1951 as the Seventeenth Quadrennial Assembly of the Student Volunteer Movement was about to open at the University of Kansas in Lawrence.

As the director of the drama, I had come early, before the arrival of the cast, to get acquainted with the stage, and to confer with those in charge of lights, sound, properties and makeup. The play, *In His Hands* by Archie Crouch, was to be premiered on the third day of the gathering. The cast would be mostly Korean students studying in seminaries and universities across the United States. Many were studying under the auspices of various denominations, and their task was to bring to life this story of the response of the Korean church to the conflict that had swept in on them from forces entirely beyond their control during the Korean War.

The major property needed for the play was a jeep. When I finally found the student in charge of properties, I was dismayed over the news that no jeep had been found and that, in frustration, he had resorted to a cardboard facsimile, which I found very ineffective.

What to do? Between rehearsals, I began searching anew for a jeep. Finally, someone thought of a nearby U.S. Army base, so I called the commanding officer. After a good bit of blustering at the other end of the line, the officer realized, I thought, the importance of the gathering at Lawrence of three thousand students, and he promised to send a jeep.

The day of the play came. We had the dress rehearsal, still imagining the presence of a real live jeep. Finally, in desperation, I called the commanding officer.

"Credit has been given on the program and all the world will know," I said. "It will be a disgrace to the whole U.S. Army if you fail to produce a jeep. A promise is a promise!" I pleaded.

Just ten minutes before the curtain was to go up, the jeep roared up and moved inside through the big doors at the rear of the stage. The day was saved and the curtain rose to a very successful performance.

Later, I asked myself, "Why did I think it would be simple to borrow a jeep from the U.S. Army? Why do I think that everything is possible, whatever the impact on the nervous systems of my friends, myself—and even total strangers?"

The questions are still unanswered!

OLD IN YEARS, YOUNG IN SPIRIT

One of my clearest and most impressive memories as a staff member of the Presbyterian Board of Foreign Missions during the 1950s is the annual birthday party for Dr. Arthur Judson Brown, from the year he was 100 years old until the year of his death when he was 106.

He had been the foreign secretary for the Board from 1895

to 1929, and was a very compelling figure in the Presbyterian Church. A birthday party for Dr. Brown, at a hotel near the Board offices, had become an annual occurrence, and his successor, Dr. Charles T. Leber, always presided. Dr. Leber's impressive introduction was matched by Dr. Brown's clarity, memory and humor. After every birthday party, we were reminded to read Dr. Brown's masterpiece, *One Hundred Years*—a unique contribution to Presbyterian mission history.

I had never before known anyone who had lived beyond a hundred years, and I was impressed by the strong voice, the articulate speech and the humor of the man as we celebrated his special day each year.

On the last of these occasions, Eleanor, his faithful daughter and companion over the years, said to me, "Father was very talkative this morning. He spoke about the Ecumenical Conference of 1900, which he organized and which was attended by over one hundred thousand people. He was very pleased to have had three U.S. presidents on the platform."* Then, smiling gently, she said, "But he also told me how disturbed he was at people's inability to understand the word *ecumenical*. He said, 'People are always misstating it as *economical*.'"

This was both amusing and amazing to me, for my colleagues and I were having the same problem still in the 1950s as we moved away from the term *foreign* missions to that of *ecumenical* mission and relations.

One sentence stands out from the occasion of his 106th birthday. "My clock," he said, "points to an evening hour, but morning is in my heart."

I said to myself, "I want to remember that for the rest of my life."

---

* The World Ecumenical Missionary Conference was held in New York in April 1900. Dr. Brown was one of the organizers and was on the executive committee of the conference, which included 2,300 official delegates from forty-eight countries. Over a ten day period, 163,000 people participated. The major evening events were held at Carnegie Hall. The three presidents were William McKinley, Theodore Roosevelt and William Henry Harrison.

WEDDING BELLS—INDONESIAN STYLE

Planning Christmas celebrations for foreign students at the Gilmor Sloane House in Stony Point, New York became a tradition in my life. It began in 1951, when the Office of Student World Relations was launched by the Presbyterian Board of Foreign Missions, and I became the director.

Every December I filled the bedrooms of a lovely Victorian house with students from all over the world who were studying in the United States under the auspices of the Board.

The moment in time that emerges from a stream of memories of merry Christmases at Stony Point is the wedding weekend of Noramah and Sumardi Reksopoetranto from Indonesia. In the midst of memories of the biblical first Christmas and celebrations of Christian customs from all over the world, came this special event of uniting two members of the group in holy matrimony.

On Christmas day, Noramah sat by the beautiful "Peace Be to This House" fireplace, weaving fresh white flowers into a lei for the groom to wear at the day-after-Christmas wedding. Every person present was involved in a wedding task. Some transformed the little Stony Point church with white flowers, candles and ribbons; some prepared to be in the wedding party. Noni Espino, who had a powerful baritone voice, was to sing. Others prepared for the wedding reception, to be attended by many Indonesians from the New York City area. In fact, several black limousines found their way to Stony Point, bringing many of the Indonesian embassy staff, of whom most were Muslim. In the midst of the reception, I remember trying to explain to the Muslim guests how the Christian brothers and sisters from around the world had become the family circle of these two young people whose own parents and siblings were far across the world in Indonesia.

Two days after the big weekend, I was waiting to board a plane at the Philadelphia airport. I realized that the person ahead of me was Indonesian, so when he turned his head in my

direction, I greeted him with "You are Indonesian, I believe."
"How did you know?" was his reply. "Oh," I said, "over the
weekend I helped two young people from Indonesia with their
wedding . . ." With surprise written all over his face, he
interrupted my explanation to say, "Then you must be that
Margaret Flory!"

It turned out that he and the groom were fellow students
and close friends at the University of California at Berkeley,
and he had heard all about the wedding.

Yes, it's a small, small world!

STOP THE PLANE! I WANT TO GET ON!

So many stories have been told about my stopping the plane in
Cebu that I think I had better describe the incident as I recall
it after some forty years.

Before boarding the Philippine Airlines plane in Dumaguete
for Manila, I received a telegram from Paul Dotson (then a
missionary student pastor in the Manila area) saying that a
Filipino youth worker would be waiting to see me during a
stopover in Cebu. After a brief conference with the young
woman in question I was waiting near the gate when Dr. Joseph
McAnliss saw me. A Presbyterian missionary doctor, he cried
out, "Why didn't the Board let us know you were coming?"

After a few pleasantries, he said, "You've got to see the new
hospital rebuilt after the war from Presbyterian Restoration
funds. I'll take you in my Jeep."

"I can't leave the airport," I protested.

He reassured me, "They always have long layovers, and the
visit will take only five minutes." Taking me by the elbow, he
rushed me to the Jeep, much against my better judgment.

After making a quick trip through the hospital wards and
meeting the doctors and nurses who were at their posts, I
returned to the front steps of the hospital only to find that Dr.
McAnliss had gone on an errand. One of the doctors called a

taxi, but before it could arrive, the Jeep roared up and I climbed in. As we drove pell-mell toward the airport, scattering pigs and chickens from the road, I realized my very precarious situation. I was going to miss five appointments in Manila that day as well as the plane to Bangkok the following morning.

As we drove into the airport, the plane's propellers were revolving and I could see that the cabin door was closed. I dashed from the Jeep and ran directly to the field in front of the cockpit. Looking up at the surprised pilot, I called out against the noise of the plane, "I've got to get to Manila! I've got to get to Manila! Please, please!!"

A man in a white suit, probably the airport manager, ran out. Signals were exchanged and the workers rolled the steps back in place. The door slid open and I rushed onto the plane. As I buckled myself into the seat, the stewardess asked, "Miss Flory, wherever have you been?" All I could think to say was, weakly, "I've been to the hospital."

As I settled into my seat, first a prayer of gratitude and then a lecture came to mind.

The prayer: "Thank you, God, that this happened in Cebu and not in New York City."

The lecture: "To M.F.: Today you overdid the Asian timing. Never again!"

PHILIPPE MAURY: APOSTLE OF JOY

When I attended my first General Assembly of the World Student Christian Federation in 1953 in Nasrapur, India, Philippe Maury, a genial French lay theologian, was the general secretary and acknowledged leader of the worldwide ecumenical movement. At that time, I was working for the Office of Student Work (later known as Student World Relations) of the Presbyterian Church.

Being one of a handful of delegates from the United States, I decided to interpret the event through a taped recording to be sent to all Presbyterian colleges and student centers. To facilitate the plan, Ben Viloria, a Filipino audiovisual specialist, having completed a study program in the United States, stopped over in India and came to Nasrapur to do the technical work on his way back to the Philippines.

There being no such thing as a soundproof area in that part of the world, the recording was made out in the open, with Philippe telling the story. During the process, crows flew into the scene, and their cawing is clearly audible. I am not sure what effect the record had in ecumenical education on the campuses, but one thing I know for certain: it had a profound effect on Philippe's small son of five, who, I was told, played it over and over again when his father was away on ecumenical journeys in Asia, Africa, Latin America or the United States.

In watching Philippe in action, I was always mindful of whence he came. The son of a French ecumenical leader, Pastor Pierry Maury, himself an early leader of the World Student Christian Federation, and as part of the resistance movement in World War II, Philippe faced political choices in which his life was at stake. He was not a professional theologian but his theological leadership astounded us.

Politics and Evangelism by Philippe Maury was a life-changing book for students from many parts of the world. For me it provided a base of understanding for ecumenical Christian action. In the foreword to the English edition of 1959, Philippe wrote: "In writing this book, I have hoped that it might be useful to men and women in the Church who, like myself, are concerned with the problems posed for them by politics and who are groping for the way to fulfill their evangelistic responsibility in faithfulness for the sake of the world."

Philippe made a trip to the United States just as the planning committee for the Eighteenth Quadrennial Student Conference on the Christian World Mission was attempting to formulate a theme. In answer to my question, "Philippe, what should this conference be about?" he strode up and down the office, pondering as he spoke. What I remember was the emergence of "two words for these times—*revolution* and *reconciliation*." After long and lively discussion by a planning committee of seventy people, we put them together as our theme.

In December 1955, Philippe came back across the Atlantic for the Quadrennial, when almost four thousand students from ninety-eight countries gathered at Ohio University in Athens, around the theme "Revolution and Reconciliation," which featured the role of the Gospel of Jesus Christ in a world heaving with change. Philippe himself was at the conference, playing a major role on behalf of WSCF and its member movements.

When a cruel illness struck and he died in 1966 at the age of fifty, the Philippe Maury Memorial Fund was launched in his memory, providing a new home for the federation as the old chalet at 13 Rue Calvin was remodeled into new apartments. Philip Potter, then the chairman of the federation, asked me to be in charge. It was a task I accepted thankfully, because of what Philippe Maury had meant to several student generations and to me.

In the end, one might say that it was the joyousness of his personhood that made Philippe such a memorable figure to all who knew him. Asian theologian D. T. Niles said it this way in the brochure that launched the Philippe Maury Memorial Fund: "If there is one word which describes Philippe, both as a man and as an executive, it is the word 'joy.' He enjoyed his work; even enjoying its problems. He enjoyed food and fun. He enjoyed his family, his friends—indeed, he enjoyed people as people. He enjoyed the rub of ideas. But above all, he enjoyed his faith. He was really happy that he had found faith in Jesus Christ. It kept him buoyant to the end."

A HOLY MOMENT

I have always thought of the "kiss of peace" as an ecumenical gift from the Church of South India to the whole of the Christian world. I first experienced it in Madras, India in 1953. At the conclusion of an event for students of the Indian Student Christian Movement, some of us participated in a worship service of the newly formed United Church of South India, which brought Anglicans, Methodists and Reformed Church members together in a new union.

The moment in time came toward the end of the service with the simple passing of the kiss of peace: One pair of hands together in prayer formation; a second pair opening to receive and embrace the first pair of hands. "May the peace of God enfold you," said the first person, and the second echoed, "And you." It was a holy moment for me that I will cherish forever.

Over the years, I have included this simple blessing in almost every service of worship I have planned. I might add that I have received the kiss of peace in a variety of ways: a big hug, a kiss on each cheek, a slap on the back, both hands clasped and so on. But the rare authenticity of that South India ceremony will remain with me always as a true and powerful gift.

"THANK YOU, DR. SOCKMAN"

Before my first visit to India, I had never heard of Fatehpur Sikri, a capital city during the Mughal period, which eventually had to be abandoned because of the impossibility of maintaining a water system. Throughout the centuries, it has stood in dinosaur fashion, stirring the curiosity of millions of tourists.

A major focus of interest at Fatehpur Sikri is a large red-clay bathtub on a pedestal in an open courtyard. Originally the bath was built for a queen. I had a chance to see this strange marvel in the company of some missionary friends on one of those side trips arranged for our ecumenical delegation, which was in Asia for five months in 1952. One member of our party suggested that I pose on the pedestal for a picture. I obliged by doing just that.

It was a good vantage point for viewing the surrounding grounds and buildings so I stayed long enough to view the landscape. But when I was ready to descend, I found it was not as easy a jump as I had thought. There was no ladder, and my friends had moved on.

Out of nowhere, it seemed, a tall man moved into sight. Sensing the situation, he held out his arm and called, "Jump!"

I did, and came face to face with Dr. Ralph Sockman, the pastor of the New York Park Avenue Methodist Church, who in those days was recognized as one of the great preachers in the country.

"Why, Dr. Sockman," I uttered in surprise, as he set me firmly on the ground. He was as surprised to have me call him by name as I was to see him, since he was not a part of my group.

Six years later, when the new Interchurch Center opened at 475 Riverside Drive in New York, I chanced to pass the large reception lounge on the first floor just as a huge portrait of Dr. Sockman was being hoisted into place. Through all the years of my service in that building and, since my retirement, on visits, I have enjoyed nodding my head to Dr. Sockman and thanking him under my breath for a gallant rescue from the queen's bathtub at Fatehpur Sikri.

BUILDING INVISIBLE BRIDGES

When the Office of Student World Relations was launched by the Presbyterian Church in 1951, I was invited to put my own ideas into action in setting up the office and recommending the program.

In the 1950s, students were described in popular journalism as having "minds as quiet as mice." Finding that they did not readily respond to speeches about mission or literature on mission, I sought new ways of getting them involved. (Looking back, I realize that "involvement" was a favorite word of mine.)

When I read about three leading colleges—Vassar, Middlebury and Sweet Briar—having junior-year-abroad students in European universities, I thought, why not send students from the church colleges and student centers to colleges overseas, especially in Asia and the Middle East? I had spent some time in those parts of the world and knew immediately the institutions I would like to approach with this idea. I envisioned the students living among the people, learning a new language, adapting to a new (perhaps less affluent) culture, learning to cross bridges of difference.

In due time I had a descriptive paper in hand to share with staff and with a special advisory committee chaired by Dr. Howard Lowry, president of the College of Wooster.

When I presented my proposal, there was stunned silence. Finally, Katherine McAfee Parker raised her voice. "Margaret," she said, "you don't know what you'll be letting yourself in for. They'll get sick, they'll fall in love, their parents will call you long distance!" She was right. All those things happened the first year.

But nothing would hold back the tide of internationalization that began sweeping the world in the early postwar years, when travel in all directions was possible once more and the "one world" dream was being pursued.

In 1953, as a part of a worldwide youth emphasis year, I traveled to colleges and universities in Asia, the Middle East and Europe to talk with their administrators about receiving students as JYAs (Junior Year Abroad students). Though other colleges were beginning to adopt JYA programs, ours was the first such plan to operate outside Europe. The chancellor of the University of Allahabad in India listened to me carefully, and then cordially assured me that he was ready to cooperate. When I left his office, I discovered that in addition to the usual information for my book of addresses, he had written: "The time has come to synthesize East and West and construct the House of Peace."

In the 1960s, the church's JYA program was expanded to include schools in Africa and Latin America. By the time the tenth anniversary of the program was celebrated in 1963, 374 students from 112 U.S. schools and colleges had participated in twenty-nine institutions in fourteen countries. They were building invisible bridges such as those described by May Sarton in her poem, "Innumerable Friend":

> Build an invisible bridge from mind to mind
> Swung out from letters or the briefest meeting:
> (Lives have been changed by a simple greeting.) *

UNDER THE BANYAN TREE

In January 1953, I arrived at the WSCF General Assembly in Nasrapur, India with a special commission in my purse. It was a letter from Friendship Press addressed to Chandran Devanesen, professor of history at Madras Christian College in Tambaram. As a poet, Dr. Devanesen was being asked to submit a selection of his poems for a volume to be published in the United States for the ecumenical mission study on India, Pakistan and Ceylon, scheduled for 1954–55.

On the second day of the assembly, I delivered the letter and then waited for a response. Soon after, Chandran appeared with a cardboard box filled with poems. Knowing the selection was being left to me, he said, "Take your choice. Try to choose the ones that Americans will want to read."

---

* May Sarton, *Cloud, Stone, Sun, Vine: Poems Selected and New* (New York: W. W. Norton & Co., 1961). Copyright © May Sarton.

With this instruction in mind, I withdrew to the shade of an old banyan tree to read. As I read, the area in South India that I was seeing for the first time became very real to me.

This moment in time under the old banyan tree in Nasrapur yielded a remarkable book entitled *The Cross Is Lifted*, as well as a remarkable new friendship.

In India, Chandran was known not only as a poet but as a leader of the Indian Student Christian Movement, as the beloved professor at Madras Christian College, as the pioneering educator who developed a new university, Northeastern Hill at Shillong, and as an ecumenical Christian leader. In the United States among Presbyterians, he was known as the one who assisted the Board of Foreign Missions in going forward in the 1950s with an innovative fine arts program. This included a major film and the development of the Barn Playhouse at Stony Point. To all his American friends, he was known for the marvelous poems he sent at Christmas that related the story of the first Christmas in Bethlehem to what was currently being experienced in the world.

At a time when the world was first facing the challenge of computers, he wrote this prayer poem:

O Lord,
As we kneel beside your crib this Christmas
Programme your love into our computerized minds
And our technicalized hearts
Till our machine-like souls
Receive again the shattering message
That God the Father wants us to explore
The vastness of His concern for all mankind,
So that the joy of His Incarnation
May dance like a beam of light from star to star
And heart to heart.

INDIA'S MAN FOR ALL SEASONS

Although I have set foot in India seven different times in my life, it was in New York City that the impact of India first hit me, all wrapped up in the person of the Reverend Augustine Ralla Ram. He was one of the three members of the Indian Team that had come to the United States at the invitation of the Presbyterian Board of Foreign Missions, of which I was a brand new staff member in 1946. I had been given some responsibility for planning and hosting a testimonial dinner at a hotel near the 156 Fifth Avenue headquarters of the Board. It was a marvelous time for a new staff member to look at our churches through Asian eyes, and I have never forgotten the sensation. Perhaps, in later years, this helped me to be sensitive to the waves of foreign students who came to our shores.

At that time, two years before the advent of the World Council of Churches, I did not know much about the movement for Christian unity in the Protestant world, but the need for such a movement was epitomized by this description from Dr. Ralla Ram. "We went into your medium-sized towns, and what did we find? Twelve churches, with twelve pastors, twelve janitors, twelve coal bills. What a waste of Christian energy!"

I thought he was the most charming man I had ever met, and the fact that he had been, in his youth, the general secretary of the Student Christian Movement of India endeared him to me. It was not too surprising that when I made my first visit to the Student Christian Movement of India six years later, Dr. Ralla Ram was in Allahabad as host and advisor.

His humor was a constant delight. When he called to invite me to share a meal with him, and I had to say no because I was scheduled for all meals for the remainder of my visit—even for breakfast—his quick reply was, "The next thing we know they will be scheduling you for bed tea" (that quaint Indian custom of waking a person up with a cup of tea at the crack of dawn!).

In India I learned of his long and persistent work toward unifying the churches. When the United Church of North India finally came into being in 1970, he was no longer living, but he was rightly credited as being one of the architects of church unity in India, and I knew that he had found his laboratory in the Student Christian Movement.

WERE YOU THERE?

Sometimes it seems incongruous to me that Rosa Page Welch and I were once a team, traveling through Asia under the auspices of Church Women United. True, she was my first black American friend, with strong bonds formed at a youth conference in Lakeside, Ohio in the late 1930s when she was a leader and I a young person from my local church. But we were an unlikely team. She sang like a nightingale, and I could not even carry a tune. (I have never quite gotten over the awful humiliation of my early grade school years when, during singing classes, I had to sit with a group of unruly boys who also could not sing on key!) Even so, anyone watching me and Rosa together or hearing our program would probably have said that we were a remarkable team!

From Thailand to India to Pakistan to Lebanon to Jerusalem, we traveled to meet with groups of high school and college students. Before an audience, Rosa would go first, describing the spirituals and their power, dividing them into songs of sorrow and songs of joy, then singing samples of each group. She ended with a song that expressed her mood of the moment. I was always fascinated with her choices. It was a bit scary for me, for I had to fit in with her mood as I spoke out of my own heart and with my own message. Then at the end, she would sing again, always sending the audience out uplifted in spirit. One spiritual that always stirred me deeply ended with the promise, "I'm gonna live so God can use me anywhere, anytime."

On this journey of about three months, there were two moments that will never leave me.

On Christmas Eve 1952, we went into a small, simple chapel in Mainpuri, India where local worshipers were holding what was for them a traditional service, but for us was gloriously different. The robes of Indian cloth were vibrant and rich in color and texture. The Christ candle at the creche and the candle brackets at the side walls of the chapel gave just enough light. Rosa sang two carols I had never heard, which became my favorites for the rest of my life: "Go Tell It on the Mountain" and "O Mary, Whatya Gonna Name That Pretty Little Baby." When the service was over, we left the church silently, lighted candles in hand. When we reached a large courtyard, bordered by many bungalows, we saw that the whole neighborhood was ablaze with light—small individual lights on the flat roofs, on the stairs, and on every window sill.

This is where Rosa's skill of choosing the right song came into play. Without a word to anyone, she strode into the middle of the courtyard, flung back her head and sang with passion: "This little light of mine, I'm gonna let it shine, . . . let it shine, let it shine, let it shine."

At the end of our journey, some two months later, we were in the Garden of Gethsemane in Jerusalem. We sat in silence on a bench, each savoring memories of the biblical stories that rushed back into our thoughts, and once again, Rosa sang the song of her choice—"Were You There When They Crucified My Lord?" Yes, I felt that I had been there, and I knew that I would never again hear that spiritual without remembering that day and that voice.

Margaret in the 1940s when she served as director of the Westminster Foundation at Ohio University.

The Rev. Tamaki Uemura of Japan, Margaret's "adopted" mother.

Margaret arrives in Korea in 1948 on the first of many trips to Asia.

The book and doll that served as messengers for peace from Margaret's Japanese students to Christian students in Japan's former enemy countries.

Margaret shares a laugh with Santa Claus (Charlie Leber) and Margaret Shannon.

The cast of *In His Hands* at the University of Kansas in Lawrence in December 1951.

Margaret's brother Fred and his wife Helen hold figurines from Japan of the old man and woman who sweep the beach at night as a symbol of married happiness.

The first International Christmas at Gilmor Sloane House, Stony Point Center, is celebrated in 1950.

Members of the 1973 WSCF General Assembly, en route to Ethiopia's royal palace for an interview with Emperor Haile Selassie.

Margaret Shannon speaks at Margaret's retirement dinner at Riverside Church in 1980.

Unveiling the plaque at the John Knox International Reformed Center in Geneva at the dedication of the Margaret Flory Conference Hall in 1993.

Dr. Richard Ferrin (right), former president of Maryville College, and Dr. Scott Brunger, professor of economics, stand with the new honorary Doctor of Humane Letters.

AIRPORT ENCOUNTER IN INDIA

One night in the late 1950s, I chanced to wait out several hours on a cozy vine-covered veranda attached to the airport in Nasrapur, India, on my way, I think, to Delhi. My mind was filled with the images of India I had experienced that day. A man sitting nearby in the semi-darkness of the veranda leaned forward to introduce himself. "I'm Martin Niemöller," he said, and, gesturing toward his wife, "This is Mrs. Niemöller."

Soon we were in a deep and lively conversation about the church in India, the ecumenical movement, and the German *Studentengemeinde* (Student Christian Movement). We shared much in the three hours we had together.

I knew enough about Pastor Niemöller's historic stand in Germany during World War II and his role in the developing ecumenical movement in Europe to be overwhelmed by the wonderful opportunity to get to know firsthand this remarkable church leader. In subsequent times, when I read an article of his in *The Christian Century* or heard him speak at an ecumenical gathering, I always felt as if I were listening to an old friend.

Years later, at the time of his death, the NBC television commentator, John Chancellor, paid him a remarkable tribute. He attributed to Niemöller the dictum that was very familiar to me, following World War II, although I had not previously known its origin:

> In Germany they came first for the Communists, and I didn't speak up because I wasn't a Communist. Then they came for the Jews, and I didn't speak up because I wasn't a Jew. Then they came for the trade unionists, and I didn't speak up because I wasn't a trade unionist. Then they came for the Catholics, and I didn't speak up because I was a Protestant. Then they came for me, and by that time no one was left to speak up.

HAVE PLANS, WILL TRAVEL

A telephone call came from Dick Shaull. It was the first week of January 1956. The call set in motion a journey for five international seminary students who had attended a student conference on the Christian World Mission in Athens, Ohio the previous week. Dick Shaull, author of the conference study book, *Encounter with Revolution*, and the major speaker at Athens, was at Princeton Theological Seminary for a couple of days before returning to his assignment among students in Brazil.

In the phone conversation, he told me he had just talked to a brilliant Argentine student, Beatriz Melano, who had presented a plan for a student-team journey to the churches of Mexico the following summer. "I told her to get in touch with you right away," Dick said, "but I thought I'd better warn you that a young tornado is coming your way."

"Dick, believe it or not, I am scheduled to be in Princeton tomorrow," I replied. "Tell her I'll meet her for lunch."

The next noon, I heard once again about the project, as enthusiasm, mixed with charm and brilliance, poured forth from the Argentine student. The Athens conference had advocated ecumenical action, and a group of Princeton students were ready to respond—three men and two women representing Germany, Chile, the United States and Argentina. Their church backgrounds were Reformed, Presbyterian and Lutheran. I held my breath as Beatriz described the proposal including the lease or purchase of a van, a preparatory study program for the spring months, and finally the visits to small church communities across Mexico. Being the chair of the Ecumenical Conference Planning Committee, I was indeed vulnerable, for this was exactly what we had hoped and prayed would happen—students responding at the grass roots to the call of mission.

I was impressed with Beatriz, with her would-be colleagues and with the plan itself. And so an operational link was formed between the Student World Relations office in New York (my base of mission and service) and an eager band of international students in Princeton. In due time, there was response from the church authorities in Mexico, and the word was "go."

For me, it was the beginning of a Beatriz watch: through marriage and the coming of children, through work with the Argentine Student Christian Movement and the assignment to a teaching post at the ecumenical seminary in Buenos Aires, and through her struggle toward a doctorate, the writing of books and eventually emerging as an original and creative theologian—an important voice on the Latin American scene.

On a day in September 1988, she was to address faculty and students at the opening convocation of a new academic year at Princeton Seminary. She had come early to the United States to visit her daughter Gabriela, a volunteer in mission stationed at Stony Point, and stayed a few days at Gilmor Sloane House where I was serving at the time as the program director. As I watched the speech in preparation and then accompanied her to Princeton, my mind went back to the telephone call from Dick Shaull that had set in motion the ecumenical journey of Beatriz Melano Couch.

A SURPRISE GIFT

Early in the summer of 1956, I received a letter from a Korean pastor who was studying in the United States under the scholarship program of the Presbyterian Board of Foreign Missions. When the day's mail was put before me, I read the letter with growing consternation. Although I no longer have the original copy, I remember the contents very clearly. It read like this:

Dear Miss Flory,
I realize that you will be leaving for Europe very soon for some
ecumenical meetings, and before you go, I want you to have a
present from me. All week long, I have been looking for a dress
for you, but I have been somewhat confused by style and color.
Because I could not decide, I am asking you to do it for me.
Enclosed is my gift of $30 to cover the cost.

My first impulse was to rush next door into the office of my
colleague, John Coventry Smith, then staff person for Japan
and Korea, who upon reading the letter laughed uproariously.

"Don't look so tragic," he said. "Just be grateful he didn't
find one."

"But, John, what will I do about the money?"

"Well, you can't send it back. He would be very offended.
You had better think creatively about using it, and send him
a graceful note of acknowledgement."

That is exactly what I did. I wrote a note of gratitude,
telling him that my wardrobe was in place before his letter
came. I told him that I would be spending some time in
Tutzing, Germany for the General Assembly of the WSCF and
would possibly be able to purchase some Bavarian woodcarv-
ings. Having longed for creche figures for the international
Christmas at the Gilmor Sloane House at the Stony Point
Center, I told him that his thoughtful gift would be applied to
the cost of carved replicas of the Holy Family.

This was one of the happiest bits of shopping I ever did
abroad. To this very day, the Bavarian creche carvings come
out of their box every Christmas to grace the mantle at the
Gilmor Sloane House, and the story of the original gift is
always appealing. Strangely enough, the creche to house the
figures was created by another Korean who was in residence at
Stony Point in the early 1980s.

Just before his death in 1984, Dr. Smith, who by that time
was general secretary emeritus of the church's Commission on
Ecumenical Mission and Relations, paid a visit to Gilmor

Sloane for an evening of reflections. The next morning, after breakfast, we exchanged a host of memories of our days together at the Presbyterian headquarters, both at 156 Fifth Avenue and 475 Riverside Drive in New York. When I repeated the story of the Korean gift, he laughed just as infectiously as he had the first time.

Unfortunately, the donor never saw his gift in its Stony Point setting because he died a few years after writing me, while still quite young. But, if Stony Point is within his ken of observation, he surely must be delighted with the joy his donation has brought over the years.

NATURE'S GLORY

Late in the summer of 1959, I found myself in the south of Brazil. After a whole summer of working with fifty students, half of whom were from Brazil and the other half from the United States, I was glad to do the last five days solo while the American students, in groups of five, with Brazilian guides, fanned out in many directions from São Paulo to visit local centers of mission.

Now I was to see the beautiful Iguaçu Falls, and the anticipation was great. But nothing had prepared me for the experience! One glorious waterfall after another broke upon the scene. Just when I thought I had reached the climax of this marvelous pilgrimage, another scene of cascading water from high cliffs opened before me and I went "oo"-ing and "ah"-ing along the way. Finally, I reached the ultimate panorama of the Iguaçu Falls, which was so remarkable in its power and beauty that I found myself weeping at the glory of God's creation.

Later that day, as I signed the guest book in the old stone inn before my departure, I found that a visitor, long before my time, had voiced my sentiments. "My poor Niagara," she had written. The signature was that of "Mrs. Theodore Roosevelt."

IN REMEMBRANCE OF HAL LEIPER

When one is young, one is not ready to lose friends to death. Those who were planning the 1955 Ecumenical Student Conference on the Christian World Mission could not believe the word that cancer would prevent our beloved friend, Hal Leiper, a member of the conference planning committee, from being with us in Athens, Ohio for this event. Hal had been a close friend of mine since his seminary days, when we were both candidates for missionary service in China.

But in the 1950s, from his post as Presbyterian university pastor at Penn State University, he had been in on all the planning at every step, and many of his ideas had been incorporated into the program. He had written the preparatory prayer guide being used on the campuses during the fall, but now he had to keep in touch from a hospital bed. Sometimes he called Athens in the middle of the night, when the drugs wore off and he was wide awake. He seemed to live the conference with us day by day.

After the conference was over, I kept in touch by phone with Hal's wife, Jane. The idea grew on me that I must see Hal once more to tell him more about the conference, to ask his counsel on a new plan I had just formulated, Frontier Internships in Mission, and to say goodbye. Then a big snowfall hit the East, and all flights were grounded. I remember leaving at six-thirty in the morning on my way to the East Side airline bus terminal in New York City, only to be told that the planes were not flying. On my third visit to the terminal I was able to board the bus, which brought me to LaGuardia Airport. I eventually landed in the mountains of Pennsylvania at Huntingdon, where Jane met the plane and drove me to the hospital.

She tried to time my visit with the period when Hal would be most alert. He was very weak, but his eyes burned bright with excitement as I described the impact of the student quadrennial conference on mission and told him about the unfolding plan for Frontier Internships in Mission that would allow gifted, committed students to spend two years on a "frontier" in the life of the world "where Christian witness was absent, inadequate or irrelevant." His counsel that day played a role in the development of this exciting program of the 1960s that still survives in the 1990s as a viable opportunity for young people in all parts of the globe.

Hal's homegoing a few days after I had made the visit was my first encounter with the death of a contemporary. Holding onto life and cherishing it to the very end was a challenge to his family and friends. Included in his preparation for the "Great Passage" was the making of a tape for his children—Scott, Heather, Margie and Paul—to be shared with them in later years.

It was natural to ask the question of God, "Why Hal? Why now!" But when I was tempted to question the eternal selection process, my temporary negativity was swept away by the reflection, "How lucky I am to have known Hal Leiper."

THE 1960s

————— ❖ —————

CHANGE ALL AROUND

LUNCH COUNTER SIT-INS

As I look back at my life and work over many years, I marvel at how often I happened to be in the right place at the right time to observe history in the making. This was surely true in February 1960 when I visited Johnson C. Smith University, a predominantly black institution in Charlotte, North Carolina. I was to be the guest of Dean Arthur George whose son, Bryant, had fulfilled a student work assignment at Forman Christian College in Pakistan under the auspices of my office a few years earlier.* Mrs. George was a leader among Presbyterian women at local and regional levels, so I felt very much at home. "Before you think of unpacking," Dean George said, "I want you to know what is happening on our campus today. Some students are sitting-in at a downtown lunch counter."

---

* Bryant George later became an executive with the United Presbyterian Board of National Missions. During the Carter administration he was appointed director for the United States Agency for International Development in Pakistan, Nepal, and the Philippines.

Then he filled me in on what had happened at a Woolworth's store in Greensboro a few days earlier when four freshmen from North Carolina A&T College had staged the first coffee counter "sit-in" of the civil rights movement. He then described the impact of that event on the Johnson C. Smith students. I remember going with him later in the day to what would now be called a "debriefing," as the students told what it was like to wait to be served and eventually to be arrested.

After more than thirty years, the details of their report have slipped away, but I do remember the dramatic sense of something new happening: a "times they are a-changin'" mood that things would never be the same in Charlotte or any other southern city. Like a firestorm, the idea of sit-in resistance spread from campus to campus across the South.

From Charlotte, I traveled directly to St. Mary's of the Spring retreat center, near London, Ohio, for the meeting of the Central Committee of the National Student Christian Federation. From the beginning of the first session, the mood was electric with excitement over what had been happening on southern campuses in North Carolina and Tennessee. It turned out that several members of the Central Committee had been involved in some of the demonstrations. The NSCF office in New York had been contacted by students in Nashville, who had requested NSCF intervention on behalf of those arrested students and the cause they represented.

The docket prepared for the NSCF meeting ahead of time was set aside and full attention was given to the issue of segregation as revealed in the sit-ins. The phones were in full service, with calls going to campus groups involved with the sit-ins and calls coming from them. I remember especially the contacts with civil rights leader Jim Lawson of Nashville.

Allan Burry,* president of NSCF, was in charge of the sessions, and much of the round-the-clock drafting of commu-

---

* Allan Burry later became the national director of higher education for the United Methodist Church. He died in 1993.

nications was done by NSCF member Bruce Rigdon.* The final result was a letter from the Central Committee to Christian students and Campus Christian Student groups in the United States. First the letter expressed "a deep concern for, and involvement with, the recently initiated and now wide-spread student demonstrations, which are seeking the end of discriminatory lunch-counter policies in stores and public buildings." The reader was reminded that "incidents growing out of the demonstrations have thrust before us, in some cases violently, important considerations such as our relationship as Christians to law and civil order, civil disobedience and passive resistance, and academic freedom and responsibility."

The letter continued: "As Christian students, our response to these turbulent events is founded in the Gospel of Jesus Christ—the knowledge that God has acted in the world." In the sit-in events, the students saw "God's judgment upon us; we are humbled before Him;" and in that judgment, they recognized "His abundant mercy in Christ and His initiative in the ministry of reconciliation."

The student leaders made plain that they were not simply seeking "the realization of American democratic values, but that they were witnessing to the fact that Christ died to reconcile all men [sic] to each other and to God."

After sharing a full summary of the affirmations regarding the recent events, they wrote: "We close, urging you as fellow Christian students to inform yourselves concerning these events, to pray for all of those involved, and to search for avenues by which you may creatively participate in this work of God in our midst."

* Bruce Rigdon, currently pastor of Memorial Presbyterian Church, Grosse Point, Michigan, was the first Bi-National Servant, the term used to describe persons who had served the church over an extended length of time in at least two different nations. Margaret Flory initiated the Bi-National Service program in 1970 to link together Christians who felt at home in at least two different cultures of the world. Its purpose was to provide community, sharing of resources, enrichment and continuing service around the world, as needs and opportunities arose.

This letter to Christian students was sent to student leaders throughout the country. I remember sending it to the missionary student pastors abroad and to the overseas churches.

Many of the students who were involved from the beginning of the civil rights movement had been at the 1959 Ecumenical Student Conference on Frontiers, in Athens, Ohio, with its emphasis on inquiry and involvement. That conference had ended with Martin Luther King, Jr. and Bola Ige of Nigeria issuing the call for racial justice. On their journey home, one busload of students had attempted to integrate a restaurant. All this and many other events had been forerunners of what was to come in the spring of 1960. It was now clear that Christian students would not be "balcony Christians" in the racial struggle unrolling daily in the United States. Many would respond to the call for action, and many would pay a price for Christian conscience and commitment.

Being with the students, black and white, in that stance for freedom and justice was to make an indescribable impact upon my ministry from that time forward.

ALL ABOARD IN PARIS—NOT!

As I write this page, it is Bastille Day in France, and the chance reference to it on television this morning brought back a memory from Bastille Day in Paris: July 12, 1960.

A delegation of fifty from the United States—students, faculty and campus minister—was on its way to a World Teaching Conference in Strasbourg, several hours from Paris by train. The conference was sponsored by the World Student Christian Federation and I was the organizing staff person for the U.S. delegation.

Being in Paris on Bastille Day, when there is dancing in the streets, was very exciting. But I had warned all our travelers to meet under the big clock in the Paris railway station at a certain time so that we could count noses before boarding the train.

Complications in our carefully worked out plans came a few days before departure when I was asked to include in our travel arrangements a delegation of eight from the Student Christian Movement of Puerto Rico.

The Puerto Rican students were alerted about departure time and requested to join the delegates from the United States under the big clock. When it was time to board the train, however, there was no Puerto Rican delegation in sight.

What to do?

When all the U.S. delegates except myself were in their seats, I waited by the train steps for the tardy ones, informing the conductor of my plight as best I could with my limited French. If I stayed in Paris to find them, I would miss a very important organizational meeting. So as the train began to move, I climbed on board, took my seat, and worried all the way to Strasbourg. What if they did not have money for overnight lodging? What if there were no reservations to be had on Bastille Day? How would they board without the group tickets which were in my purse? My mind went around and around about what to do when I got off the train in order to facilitate their travel the following day.

Late the next afternoon, the leader of the group found me to explain and apologize. They were having such a good time dancing in the streets that they had lost track of time. When they realized they had missed the train, they decided to dance the night away.

This bit of cultural exposure was good preparation for many experiences I was to have in the future, as my life work took me to Latin America. In later years, when the giddy students of the 1960s became teachers and pastors, there was much laughter in remembrance when, once again, our paths crossed.

NEVER DESPAIR

On the second day of a 1961 Ghana Study Seminar in Aburi, one of the delegates, a young woman from Minnesota, became desperately ill and was rushed to a hospital in Accra. Loneliness and anxiety encompassed me as I waited outside the door of the room where the young student, Carol, lay in an out-of-mind state, wildly thrashing about and moaning. The tests seemed to reveal traces of typhoid, but by evening the verdict was meningitis. The attending doctor finally put into words the seriousness of the situation. "She may not live the night; you had best inform the parents." Cable was the only transcontinental means of communication in those days, and so a cable was sent.

Then my attention turned to the rest of that group of thirty students, both African and American, who were in the opening stages of a long-anticipated African Study Seminar sponsored by the National Student Christian Federation of the USA. They had to be told. Perhaps some of them had been infected in the previous ten days of traveling in West Africa. On the way up the hill from the hospital, I prayed fervently for Carol and for the waiting students.

All at once there was a great honking from a mammy wagon (a kind of open jeep) passing on the road. In the dust and the gathering twilight, I read the sign hanging in the back of the vehicle. "Never Despair," it said, and I knew those words were for me.

Upon my arrival at the conference site, Paul Verghese, our theologian in residence (now known as Metropolitan Paulus Gregorious of the Syrian Orthodox Church of India), was waiting for me. "Get the group together, please," I said. "Let me tell them about Carol. Please pray for her, and ask the students to join you."

For the next hour, the prayers poured forth for our sister Carol. When finally I fell into bed, exhausted, for the first time that day I experienced a peacefulness of heart, knowing that Carol's future was in God's hands and sensing that we might see her again.

About five in the morning, a call came from the hospital. "Miss Flory," said the nurse in charge, "Carol has made it through the night. She will live." The mood of joyous gratitude that swept over the group at breakfast stayed with us for the duration of our seminar. From her hospital bed Carol participated, interacting with the group in a variety of ways.

By the end of the seminar, she was able to travel by wheelchair, and I accompanied her as far as London. In the meantime, the African and American students who had shared a summer of joys and sorrows said their farewells and headed to their home campuses for another round of academic life. A major discovery of the summer was that although they had left Africa, Africa would never leave them.

Later I remembered a kindly man who had come to the hospital as a question mark hung over Carol's life. On the day he came, I experienced him as a faithful Presbyterian elder. But later I learned he was also the much-beloved Justice Olenu of the Supreme Court of Ghana. The faithfulness of the local Christian community was a strong sign to me of God's love in action.

A FATHER AND A SON

On a June morning of 1961, as a session of the seminar in Aburi was about to begin, I realized that a number of cars had arrived and that our meeting place was circled by security police. I sought Nicholas Anim, the African educator who, on behalf of the Student Christian Movement of Ghana, was in charge of all arrangements. To my question "Who are they?" he replied, "The security police. They are here because our morning speaker is J. B. Danquah, Nkrumah's main opposition. They will be listening in." I did not like it one bit, but I realized there was no alternative, at least not for the morning session.

I knew something about Dr. Danquah from my reading in advance of the seminar, from the opening orientation session, and from the row of books in his name in the library at the University College in Accra. He was called the George Washington of Ghana. I understood why after I heard this man of the white hair, big smile and compelling manner address the students. It was a great session, and we all felt honored by his presence—both Africans and Americans.

When I returned to the United States, I sent him the customary thank you note for his contribution, a note expressing warm enthusiasm because we had lived through some great moments in his presence. Soon after, I read in the *New York Times* that "the opposition leader," J. P. Danquah, had been imprisoned. Many of us prayed for him in the ensuing months.

About a year later, I received a note from him in which he mentioned coming out of prison and tackling a vast amount of mail that had accumulated. He had found my letter and was sending his best wishes. "You are working with the young," he wrote. "It is the most important work in the world."

Some months later I learned through the *New York Times* that he had been imprisoned again; then later, I received word of his death.

Several years later I had landed at the new airport in Accra and was walking toward the terminal with my numerous handbags when a tall, young Ghanian moved up beside me. "Is this your first trip to Ghana?" he asked. "No," I replied, "I came with a group of American students in 1961. This is a new airport—very impressive!"

"If you were here in 1961," he said, "you must have heard about my father, J. P. Danquah." I was so startled and pleased that I dropped my bags and held out both hands! In the ensuing conversation I told him about the letter, and he told me that he had come home from Addis Ababa where he had a post in Africa House with the Council of African States.

When we went through the gate, hundreds of Africans were waiting. A great shout went up, and they surged forward to surround him. Now there were two Danquahs in my book of memories.

PRAGUE 1962

It was March 1962. The letter postmarked "Prague" was a surprise to me. But the contents were even more of a surprise. I was being invited by Dr. Joseph Hromádka, through his secretary, Milan Opocensky, to attend the meeting of the Advisory Committee of the Christian Peace Conference in Karlovy Varo the following month. The remarkable coincidence was that the dates were exactly the ones I had free between two sets of World Student Christian Federation meetings in Geneva!

I made an appointment with John Coventry Smith, the General Secretary of the Presbyterian Commission on Ecumenical Mission and Relations, and introduced the matter. As I sat down by his desk, I said, "John, I think the Holy Spirit is sending me to Prague." He looked a little startled and then read the letter through without comment. I told him of the coincidence that I would be in Europe at the time. I also told him the invitation was probably the result of a friendship formed with Dr. Hromádka in Brazil at the time of the meeting of the World Alliance of Reformed Churches in 1959, and with Milan Opocensky at a meeting of the WSCF Executive Committee in Bangalore, India during the previous year. After some pondering, John said, "Yes, I think you should go—unofficially, of course. Be a listener and an observer and let us know what you see and hear."

That was the easiest assignment I had had in a long time, but getting the visa wasn't so easy. Madame Stauffer in the WSCF office in Geneva took on the task of contacting the Czech Embassy in Bern. Special persons carried the papers back and forth. I remember making one trip myself. The day before departure came, and no visa. I was to learn that there was always a cliff-hanging time before getting a visa to an East European country. But after a stream of last-minute telephone calls, it was granted. (In those days a visa was a piece of paper inserted in the passport, not a stamp on the passport.)

As I arrived and departed from a gray and somber airport, it was clear to me that the Cold War was at its height. There was a bus to take the delegates from the airport into the city, and when I stepped down from the bus onto the streets of Prague, there, waiting for me, was a lady of patrician stance who introduced herself as Julia Matouskava.

Valdo Galland, general secretary of the WSCF, had told me about her in Geneva. She was a former general secretary of the Czech Student Christian Movement who had asked the Geneva staff to send into Czechoslovakia, with any person coming into the country, copies of *The Student World*, because the publication was not permitted entry by regular mail. Needless to say, I was the courier.

Julia handed me a nosegay of violets, saying, "You are going to have tea with me. I have official permission." And so, over the next hour and a half in a Czech tearoom, I heard about the life of the World Student Christian Federation in Czechoslovakia "between the great wars."

She described her trip as a delegate to the WSCF General Assembly in Peking, China, in 1924. She had been on the ship with Valdo Galland's father, and it had taken them three months to go and return. I can still recall the tingle up and down my spinal column at the thought that twenty-five years before the beginning of the modern ecumenical movement at Amsterdam, student Christian leaders were crossing the world to attend crucial meetings of the WSCF.*

* Through the influence of the American visionary John R. Mott, the WSCF had come into existence in Vastena, Sweden in 1895, as a federation of student Christian movements.

Thus, it was quite understandable that many of the delegates to the World Council of Churches General Assembly in Amsterdam in 1948 had received their initial training in ecumenicity by attending Federation meetings.

Julia Matouskava was to remain my very dear friend until her death two decades later.

GRIEVING FROM AFAR

Sometimes events have significance far beyond their immediate meaning. In the summer of 1967, I participated in a remarkable consultation at Anderson College in Indiana, sponsored by Church Women United and organized by Margaret Shannon, then general secretary of CWU. This event brought together women from the U.S. and from overseas to plan a conference on internationalization. I was asked to chair a group on ways of working together in the future.

Our discussion was very fruitful, and then came the task of preparing the report. I was delighted with the faithfulness and stamina with which two women, Luz Ausejo from the Philippines and Shahla Anand of India, stayed with me far into the night to hone the report so that it would fully reflect the international and intercultural subtleties in our discussions.

I remember also the meaningful Sunday evening service that took the form of an "Emmaus Walk" at sunset. Each participant drew a partner by joining her strip of wood with another's to form a small wooden cross. My companion on the walk was Joyce Bailey of Jamaica. I have kept the small wooden piece all these years and remember the remarkable sharing that took place. (Years later, I was to use this same approach at the Stony Point Center to bring women together around spiritual issues on the Days of Direction, which were occasionally sponsored at Gilmor Sloane House.)

But the experience that was to take on profound significance later in my life was a conversation with Coretta Scott

King. Coretta was one of the major leaders for the Anderson Retreat. She led the evening vesper service in a beautiful and compelling way. It so happened that she and I both had to leave the conference early, which meant we were together in the back seat of a limousine for a long drive to the Indianapolis airport. After sharing such a remarkable week, it was easy for us to talk of things that were close to our hearts. She spoke a great deal about her husband, Martin Luther King, Jr., and the current nature of the civil rights struggle. She told me that he never left the house on a trip without their realizing that they might not see each other again. "This is something with which we live daily," she said simply.

I was to remember those words in the assembly of the Christian Peace Conference in Prague the following spring. Following my initial trip to Prague in 1962 in the interest of peace, I had returned in 1968. On an April morning, I entered the big meeting hall around eight-thirty in the morning, ready to start the day. A young delegate to the conference from Brazil, who saw me across the room, came over immediately to say, "Have you heard that Martin Luther King has been shot and killed?"

I cried out and covered my face. Seeing my reaction, Father Paul Verghese (Metropolitan Paulus Gregorius) quickly crossed the room, put his hand on my shoulder, and said, "Margaret, Gandhi, too, left us when we needed him most." Somehow the rejoinder from an old and trusted friend saw me through the day.

Along with all the other delegates from the United States, I tried to follow the agenda with a wounded heart. Writing a message of condolence and solidarity to Coretta Scott King and finding a way of sending it off was the only response I could think of at that moment when so many dreams were shattered in our country and all we knew in the far-off city of Prague was that fires were burning in our streets. We had lost the one person with the spiritual and moral power to lead us on.

Walking the Bamboo Carpet

Arriving in a foreign airport always brings a bit of anxiety. Will someone be there to meet me? If not, what shall I do?

This was never my concern in Manila, however. I knew there would always be friends watching and waving as I embarked from the plane.

One arrival, probably in the early 1960s, is especially memorable. The welcoming group had painted a bamboo carpet depicting the arrival of the MF (Margaret Flory) Express with greeters calling out *"Mabuhay!"* and a friendly carabao swishing his tail in greeting. A small group got closer to the plane than most non-passengers usually do and insisted on my walking the carpet—which I did in some embarrassment, ever aware of the amused glances of fellow passengers moving toward the terminal.

When the bamboo carpet was finally lifted and rolled up under the arms of Danny Aguila (now an artist/editor on the staff of the United Methodist Publishing House in Nashville) we proceeded to the checkpoints for immigration and customs.

Emerging from the customs at last, with my bags now in friendly hands, I faced a line of greeters—perhaps as many as twenty. Shaking hands and greeting each in turn, I kept glancing ahead to be sure I could pull names out of my memory bank.

All at once there was a face I had never seen; so I just smiled, shook hands and said, "Thank you for coming." Later I was glad I had not pretended I was greeting a longstanding friend, as the unknown person turned out to be someone I had never met before—a dressmaker who had come to the plane to take my measurements for the dress she was to make as a farewell gift. When a late arrival at the airport asked, "Where is Miss Flory?" one of the young pastors whom I did know well, Ely Mapanao, answered with great glee, "She is in the ladies' room having a fit." It was true, inasmuch as the dressmaker, with pins in hand and mouth, was taking my measurements.

At departure time some days later, a beautiful black and silver Filipino dress with butterfly sleeves and shawl collar appeared. I wore it proudly on special occasions until middle age set in. Now it is a part of the Margaret Flory collection of international garments housed in a closet on the third floor of the Gilmor Sloane House at the Stony Point Center.

NEW NATIONS, NEW DIPLOMATS

Arriving in Freetown, Sierra Leone is a unique experience. The national airport for this West African country is on an island off the mainland, and one travels from island to mainland in a small boat, surrounded by one's baggage. Although my chief purpose in visiting this newly independent country (only two months old in June 1961) was to contact the university and its Student Christian Movement, I also looked forward to seeing my good friends, John and Rena Karefa-Smart.

I first met John when, as a medical student from Sierra Leone, studying in Canada, he had visited Ohio University where I was in graduate school. His wife, Rena, an African American, had been an officer in the World Student Christian Federation, and we had been together in many meetings. Now they were back in Sierra Leone, where John was the foreign minister for a new nation. A small group of Sierra Leone ambassadors had been picked to be sent out to crucial spots around the world, and as a guest of John and Rena, I was invited to have dinner with them and their wives.

As we were introduced, I realized that I was familiar with all the cities to which they would be going. Soon the group of wives surrounded me, and question followed question—about food, weather, cultural opportunities, education and so forth in those places. I could not always answer in depth, but it seemed to mean so much to them that someone had actually seen these far-off places with her own eyes! And, because as a person "I am part of all that I have met," I enjoyed thoroughly summoning up the images that would help answer their questions.

The 1960s marked the time of new nationhood in Africa, and "new nationalism" was one of the frontiers to which we assigned Frontier Interns. During the ensuing years, when word appeared in the press or other media about these new countries, I thought of my friends in the circle in Sierra Leone and wondered what life was like for them in their new homes on several continents.

A DAY AT THE WHITE HOUSE

In mid-July of 1963 I received a telephone call in Princeton from the secretary of the New York office. "Margaret," India Thybulle's voice rang with excitement, "You have a telegram from President Kennedy, inviting you to the White House next Thursday."

"What?" I exclaimed excitedly. "Is it true? Read it to me!"

Yes, it was true, and a week later I was in the East Room of the White House along with three hundred other women from all fifty states and from a broad range of women's constituencies. I was included in the religious group. Even before President Kennedy came on the scene, it was thrilling to look around the room and recognize people from every part of our America, people of every race and many ethnic groups.

When the president came in, he welcomed us, he said, not only to seek support for the passage of his civil rights bill but because he felt women were a great moral force in the nation whose insights and energy were needed in the great struggle ahead. After his presentation, he paused for questions. A young black woman who was sitting down front spoke up and said, "Mr. President, I have listened very carefully, and nothing you have said will touch the situation in Mississippi."

"I understand," the young President answered sadly and gravely. "But if the rest of the nation takes hold of the situation and works as hard as it can, eventually Mississippi will catch up!"

Then President Kennedy introduced his brother Bobby, who told of a special campaign for equality among the races that the administration was waging in five hundred cities across the nation. Next, the President said he would have to leave us for a time to confer with his ambassador-at-large, Averell Harriman, who was leaving for Russia that evening. He said he hoped we would be willing to serve as his "Women's Committee on Civil Rights," and that he was requesting us to stay on in Washington through the evening. He introduced Mildred McAfee Horton, formerly president of Wellesley College, whom he had asked to chair the rest of the meeting, and Esther Peterson from the Labor Department, who would serve as staff.

Some people left to change their travel plans so that they could stay on, but since I had already planned to take the last shuttle flight back to New York that night, I did not budge from my seat. Later in the afternoon, a messenger appeared to report that President Kennedy would say goodbye to us in the Rose Garden. When we arrived there, we found the President, Vice President Lyndon Johnson, the members of the Cabinet and Averell Harriman. It was a heady moment.

In the evening, we reconvened in an auditorium in the Labor Department to carry on the discussion instituted in the afternoon. I sat forward, in the second row, to lend encouragement to Mrs. Horton, whose sister, Katherine McAfee Parker, had been a close friend of mine for many years.

On the shuttle to New York late that night, I sat between two remarkable women who had been present at the White House, and we talked about the marvelous experiences of the day all the way to La Guardia. One of them was Eleanor Holmes Norton, whose career I have followed ever since on television and in the press. One can always count on a balanced opinion from her. As I write, she is the District of Columbia's delegate to Congress.

By November of that year, the voice of John F. Kennedy was silenced forever. But in the meantime, regular mailings were addressed to the new Women's Committee on Civil Rights. Forever after, I would hold onto the memories of an incredible day at the White House, a day of substance and new hope in the country's struggle for the civil rights of all its citizens.

AN ECUMENICAL ALERT

When I join others to sing "For All the Saints," I remember Suzanne de Diétrich of France and the French Reformed Church. She was one of the first European church leaders I came to know through meetings set up by the World Student Christian Federation. Our first encounter was in 1951 at the WSCF Bible Study Conference in Kalamazoo, Michigan. As an impressive leader of Bible studies and the author of *Free Men* and *The Witnessing Community*, she was already well known on the American scene.

Our second contact was at the Chateau de Bossey, the Ecumenical Institute in Celigny, Switzerland, which I first visited in 1953. At the time a major flood in the Netherlands had occurred, and the student body at Bossey, drawn from many parts of the world, had met in the chapel for a prayer service led by Suzanne de Diétrich. It was one of my earliest experiences (there were to be countless more) of the world church at one in prayer in a moment of crisis for Christian brothers and sisters. The fact that the director of the Ecumenical Institute, Dr. Hendrick Kraemer, was from the Netherlands, added poignancy and meaning to the act of sharing a sacrificial meal and prayer together.

In 1960, at the WSCF World Teaching Conference, Suzanne was introduced to students from all over the world on the same platform with world-renowned theologians and ecumenists such as Karl Barth, W. A. Visser t'Hooft, Robert Mackie and Emil Brunner.

In 1963, in an old brick house on the campus of Princeton Seminary, members of the International Study Fellowship of the University Ministry anxiously awaited her arrival—twenty-three persons from nineteen countries, who were preparing for more effective service among students and faculty on campuses around the world.

This rich event was the culmination of years of planning and anticipation. It was a poignant moment for me also as Shirley Lewis, who had been my associate for seven years while we got the Frontier Internship off the ground and who did so much else to keep our work going, was staffing her last event before moving (after some preparation at Indiana University) to the University of Michigan, where she has done distinguished work among international students ever since.

At this time, Suzanne's health was fragile, and she was traveling with crutches. Her spirit, however, was as lively as ever. As she had done for me ten years earlier, she raised the question of how the Church continues God's purpose of being the witnessing community. She made clear that our call is to be "the Church," not only as individual members of a congregation or denominational family, but also as responsible citizens of a given country and of a wider world of nations.

Because of her participation in the French resistance movement during World War II, her words always carried prophetic meaning to any gathering of students.

The last time I saw her was in the late 1960s in Geneva, Switzerland, where I had gone to help negotiate plans for a new headquarters location for the World Student Christian Federation. The former WSCF house at 13 Rue Calvin near St. Peter's Cathedral in Geneva was being incorporated into a modern housing project, and the Federation had to find a new home. In the midst of our work, Suzanne had arrived from Paris, and it was agreed that we should interrupt our session for a conversation with her. We were seated in an informal circle, and there was someone by my side putting her French into English. All at once, Suzanne, looking over at me and realizing what was happening, stopped the flow of her comments and said in her high, penetrating voice, "Margaret Flory, an ecumenical person like you never having learned French—shame, shame!"

It was said lightly, but the point struck home. And forever after, I would urge the students with whom I worked to become proficient in more than one language. The reality of the world as a global village was breaking into my awareness, and I was already wishing that in my own youth someone had put to me so definitely the challenge of mastering at least one language in addition to my own.

DESTINATION UNKNOWN

When the World Council of Churches adjourned in Uppsala, Sweden in the summer of 1968, Margaret Shannon and I spent a short vacation in Russia, flying from Stockholm to Moscow. At this time the Cold War was very, very cold.

Although we were put in the care of a tourist travel agency, we found some moments to reconnoiter on our own. We particularly enjoyed Leningrad, and as we walked along the banks of the River Neva, we realized that a boat was about to leave from a nearby landing. Thinking it was the boat for the river trip we wanted to take, I ran ahead to get tickets, thrusting a handful of rubles at the lady in the wire cage so that she could take out what she needed. Instead of the leisurely boat trip around the city that we expected, the boat, which turned out to be a hydrofoil, headed directly out to sea. We had no idea where we were going. We could not communicate with anyone on board, nor they with us.

Eventually we arrived at a port. I do not know where it was, but we determined to stay on board in the hope of a quick return to Leningrad. Despite all our protesting, we were put off the boat, an officer pointing to a building on shore where he evidently expected us to report. Margaret thought one of us should remain near the boat, so I went in to explore.

It was a longer walk than I had anticipated, and soon Margaret was out of sight. I had no idea where I was or what I was going to do. Then I saw a long line of people and realized that they were waiting to buy tickets, so I joined them, all the time wishing there was some way of telling Margaret what had happened to me. I tried very hard, using all the tricks I knew about communicating in strange places, but the Russians in the line around me merely shook their heads.

Then an unexpected surprise transformed the day. Some African students who were studying in Russia realized I was speaking English, and they came to check on me. In a few moments, my whole situation changed. Just the week before, I had finished eight years of service as chair of the Foreign Students Committee of the World Student Christian Federation, and the idea of talking with foreign students in Russia blew my mind. This was the kind of situation Margaret always referred to as "the hook-and-eye activity of the Holy Spirit." They explained where I was and confirmed for me that I was in the right line for return tickets to Leningrad.

I told them about the recent assembly of the World Student Christian Federation in Helsinki, which I had attended earlier in the month. By this time I wanted the line to slow down so that I could prolong this marvelous conversation, for they walked the line with me to share every moment while the Russians looked on stolidly, but with some wonderment. All this time, poor Margaret was waiting down by the shore out of sight, wondering what had happened to me.

Eventually my turn came, I bought the appropriate tickets, returned to the shore, and we reboarded for our return. To say that we were relieved when the boat docked in Leningrad is an understatement, but we were also grateful for the blunder that had become a blessing.

CONSCIOUSNESS RAISING IN BOGOTA

I can remember the exact moment of my realization that a new consciousness among young women of the United States was for real. As the director of the Frontier Internship Program, I had gone to Bogota, Colombia in May 1969 to meet with the Frontier Interns from the U.S. who were serving in Latin America. My purpose was to evaluate the program and was a step in a process to internationalize the program more fully.

The time of day was late afternoon and our group was expecting guests for dinner in the apartment that had been borrowed for a long weekend. When I realized there was no activity in the kitchen, I started on a search for the women interns who were to carry the responsibility for the meals. I found them in a back room in the midst of what they called "our caucus."

"We are preparing our non-negotiable recommendations," said the spokesperson from her place on the bed. "Will you call a meeting with the men?"

Feeling a little disoriented, I said, "Yes, but please fill me in a little more." Although I had read *The Feminine Mystique* by Betty Friedan and had heard the rumblings around me, and although I had experienced for years what was now being expressed as the women's liberation movement, I was not quite prepared for the complaints that came tumbling out against spouses and the system. I remember one intern commenting, "The most radical guy among them is the least sensitive." She was referring to her husband. When I finally got the floor, I said, "All right, we will meet tonight after our guests leave, but in the meantime, will you please help with the meal?" I felt a little trapped and guilty in making this plea since I realized that a big issue was on the horizon of their consciousness as they were being called back to traditional tasks.

To put it mildly, the young men in the circle that night were amazed as they heard the recital of their insensitivities. I remember one saying feebly, "Well, I do the dishes every other week." Next, the Frontier Intern program and its director—namely me—were put on the spot, although I had an easier time since I was already on their wavelength. The first demand was "a separate frontier assignment for every woman intern." Originally couples were assigned to the same frontier. "Yes, that can be done," I answered, as my mind wondered if the committee back home would defend my promise. The second demand was for a special leader at the annual orientation program who would conduct a special briefing on women's issues. Again, my answer was in the affirmative. In the months that followed, the process we had experienced that evening in Bogota was to be called "consciousness raising."

My greatest task was in interpreting the meaning of this watershed session to the Frontier Internship Committee back in New York. But the struggle was effective. When the next group of Frontier Interns went abroad, each woman had her own frontier and all had been through an exciting session with a dynamic young feminist, Charlotte Bunch, at their orientation conference at Stony Point Center. But it was not to be all roses. Two pastors, one from Korea and one from Africa, informed me, "We don't want any liberated women assigned to our countries."

"The mills of God grind slowly." But they do grind!

PICTURE SHATTERED

I did not go to Europe with the Presbyterian Women's Fellowship Mission in 1951, but my camera did—with Margaret Shannon!

When Margaret returned, she showed me a slide of a tall, handsome African man taken at the Evangelical Seminary in Portugal. "This is Eduardo Mondlane of Mozambique," she said. "I told him about your work with international students. He may look you up when he comes to the United States."

One day two years later, I looked up from my desk at 156 Fifth Avenue in New York to see this giant of a man standing in my doorway. "Why, Eduardo," I said, "welcome to the United States."

He was astounded that someone who did not know him could call him by name. Of course, I did know him through his picture and Margaret's description, but to him it was a miracle. From that moment forward, we were fast friends.

I was in touch with Eduardo throughout his time in the United States, during his student days in Illinois, his teaching in Syracuse, and his time of service at the United Nations. Eventually he went back to Africa, taking with him his American wife, Janet, and their children. He and his wife went to work with the Mozambique Institute in Dar es Salaam, Tanzania, as a base of interpretation and action on behalf of Mozambique's movement for independence from Portugal.

I visited them there in the mid-1960s when I was arranging for an American couple to serve as Frontier Interns at the Institute. At the time I was there, Dar es Salaam was also host to a visit of the Trusteeship Council of the United Nations. Eduardo, at that time the head of Frelimo (the front for the liberation of Mozambique), and predicted to be the future president of Mozambique, was involved in meetings around the clock. He sent word that he might not be able to see me off, but then he arrived at the airport and we had a few minutes to talk before the plane was called. He wanted me to understand and help explain why Frelimo had to turn to the Soviet Union for help in their struggle.

"We have to get help towards freedom wherever we can find it," he said.

It was our last conversation. Within six months he was gone, killed by a letter bomb in his own home.

When Mozambique, through the efforts of Frelimo, finally became independent in 1975, I rejoiced in my heart that Eduardo's children would experience the freedom that Eduardo had sought for his people.

THE 1970s

———— ❖ ————

NEW DIMENSIONS

REMEMBERING D. T. NILES

On the July morning of 1970 when word reached the Interchurch Center in New York of the death of D. T. Niles of Ceylon (now Sri Lanka), calls were made to the desks of those who had known and worked with D. T. in the missionary and ecumenical movements. Within minutes, we gathered in the U.S. office of the World Council of Churches (then on the fourth floor of the Center) to remember D. T. and to thank God for his life and work.

We remembered him as the husband of Dulcie Arulratnam Niles, who accompanied him to the Second Assembly of the World Council of Churches in Evanston in 1954; we remembered him as the father of two young men whom we were beginning to know in the ecumenical movement, Preman and Dyalan; we remembered him as the lively leader of the Christian Conference of Asia and as the president of the WCC in Asia; we remembered him as the writer of a book, *That They May Have Life*, that had profoundly affected our thinking in the world of ecumenical mission.

We remembered his unique definition of evangelism—"One beggar helping another beggar find bread"—and the way he summarized the essence of the Christian faith in a few words: "When you meet the man in the road, this is what you should say: 'God made you. God loves you. God gave His Son for you. When you die, you will go to God.'"

We remembered him as the eloquent preacher who gave the opening sermons at the assemblies of the World Council of Churches in Amsterdam and in Uppsala. We remembered his prophetic insight as time after time in group after group, he helped to chart the future of the ecumenical movement.

As we shared our memories, we laughed and we cried in community and gave thanks prayerfully for the privilege of having been the friend and colleague of D. T. Niles, a "genuine original" in the gallery of ecumenical giants.

As for me, I remembered his first message to the World Student Christian Federation when he became president in 1953 at Nasrapur, India. I remembered the conversation around my appointment by D. T. at the WSCF Assembly in Salonika, Greece. It was 1960 and he appointed me the chairperson of a new Committee on Foreign Students, meaning students living in any country temporarily that was not their homeland. (Later, we were to use the term International Students.) I remembered his flashes of humor and his wonderful laugh when he was in the chair at Federation meetings. I remembered his gift of leadership to the Federation in the Life and Mission of the Church project, which dominated the life of the Federation and the Student Christian Movements for a number of years in the late 1950s and early 1960s. But most of all, I remembered a lunch over curry in Geneva in the year of his death, when he told me that his association with the World Student Christian Federation had been the most formative experience of his life.

Then he shared his hopes and apprehensions for the Federation, and recognizing me as a longtime WSCF Senior Friend and supporter, he said, "Margaret, help them to keep the center strong." I knew what he meant, for he had often talked to me about the fragmentary effect of regionalization. He fervently believed the biblical motto of the Federation, "That all may be ONE that the world may believe."

Several weeks later, in the memorial service at the Interchurch Center, I heard the eulogies of several leading U.S. Protestants, felt again the force of his faith and his commitment, and vowed to continue keeping the World Student Christian Federation in the center of my ecumenical concern. And I have done this. Now as the present WSCF leadership, with Senior Friends like myself, plan for the centennial of the Federation in 1995, I cannot help but think that D. T. must be preparing the keynote message from the gallery of ecumenical saints.

SADNESS SHARED IN COMMUNITY

The General Assembly of the World Student Christian Federation had barely convened the first week in January 1973 when word reached me that my father had died in Florida and would be taken to our home town of Wauseon, Ohio for burial. Although I had spent Thanksgiving at his bedside and had questioned the wisdom of being away from the family, my doctor brother encouraged me to proceed with the trip as planned over several months.

However, now in Addis Ababa, Ethiopia, so far from home and family, I felt a sense of shock and isolation. Accordingly, I made plans for the trip home.

But when the Ethiopian chair of the Planning Committee came to me at lunchtime with my ticket in hand, he said, "Here is your ticket, but we don't think you should go. After all, you are our family, too." A blow to the chin or a bucket of cold water in my face could not have been more compelling!

"You always talk about the world church community being your family," I said to myself, "but when a moment of crisis comes, you abandon your conviction and decide to go home."

And so I unpacked my bag and put away the ticket after calling the family in Ohio to say that I would come to them when the assembly ended two weeks hence.

The next day a memorial service for my father was held with my friends and colleagues in Addis Ababa, as a part of the morning worship led by the WSCF president, Dick Shaull. As I heard the prayers for my father from young voices in the accents of the whole world, I knew why I had stayed.

A Missionary to America

In 1973, the Presbyterian Church was in the process of being restructured. All persons on national staffs were asked to resign to facilitate the process of starting afresh. The blow for me was especially poignant as I was in the first years of an exciting assignment called "New Dimensions in Mission," a challenge to seek out those dimensions of global mission to which the denomination should give attention through education and involvement.

Then one day I was offered a post entitled "Human Resource Planning," and was placed in an alternative location, as the game of musical chairs had not yet been completed. On a particular day, I faced a desk piled high with mail that needed attention. I was halfway through the pile when I came across a letter from the Reverend John Gatu, general secretary of the Presbyterian Church of East Africa, with headquarters in Nairobi, Kenya.

John Gatu was a well known colleague, but I was quite unprepared for the contents of the letter. It was a simple announcement that the Presbyterian Church of East Africa had decided to send a missionary to the United Presbyterian Church in the United States. The East African church would pay his travel expenses and continue his salary while he was in the United States for two years. However, he wanted to bring his wife Helen and two of their six children. "Is there anything the sister church in America can do," he asked, "to provide the supplemental funds needed?"

Well, I thought, this is something new. Our church had been in the habit of receiving persons from abroad on all kinds of visits, but this was the first time a church was ready to commission a missionary to us! I felt a deep surge of excitement as I continued working my way through the pile of mail.

Before finishing work that afternoon, I found a letter from the Evangelism Committee of Hudson River Presbytery in New York State, asking for help in finding the appropriate person from an overseas church to come for a special program on evangelism, adding that $15,000 was available for this project.

I was not only surprised but elated as I clipped the two letters together! Truly, the Holy Spirit was at work at my desk on that August afternoon.

The Jacob Mugo family arrived in the early fall that year, and within the next two years of activity, reactions and questionings, a laboratory in the internationalization of mission developed. This was a first step leading to the Mission to the USA program, which, in the next twenty years, would enable several hundred persons from partner churches all over the world to come in mission to us, fulfilling my own deep conviction that the Gospel of Jesus Christ will not be fully understood until all of the world's Christians have an opportunity to share with one another what Jesus Christ means to them.

Ironically, though my new title after the restructuring sounded like it belonged more in a secular service agency than the church, in fact, I was still involved in new dimensions in mission.

The Primal Scream

What do Bainbridge in Ohio and Srinagar in Kashmir have in common? If you had asked me that question one sad night in Srinagar, I probably would have said, "Mice!"

Flashback to 1938 when I did a stint of teaching at Bainbridge High School. During a rehearsal of the junior class play, for which I was the coach, a mouse ran across the stage, whereupon I climbed onto a chair and then a table. Getting down again and gaining control over the rehearsal was a bit difficult and quite embarrassing!

The scene shifts to my homeroom a few days later. Coming into the room with an armload of books and papers, I headed to my desk. Just as I arrived and put my foot down in a final step something jumped, and I ran out of the room as the kids shouted in glee. I knew then that I had to face them again right away. So I marched back in, all eyes on me, took a clean sheet of paper from my tablet and wrapped up the cause of my fear—a rubber mouse. Taking it to the principal's office, I said, "Please lock this up. I never want to see it again."

When I went back to speak at graduation some years later, the principal opened the safe and took out the mouse. "We keep it here to remember you," he said.

1970: The scene shifts back to Kashmir, that place of romantic beauty that I had longed to visit, not because of picturesque ads in the *New York Times* travel section, but because of the fervent testimony of dear friends. The few days of gondola rides and fascinating shopping in the bazaars were over, and it was time to pack. When I opened my suitcase, the scream was primal, for there in my travel bag was a nest of squirming, helpless baby mice! My scream was answered by a room attendant who rushed in, understood the situation and carried off the offensive suitcase.

Is it any wonder that Bainbridge in Ohio and Srinagar in Kashmir became inseparably linked in my memory?

THE UNHAPPY BIRTHDAY

Seeing former Presbyterian missionary Donald Bobb at a Global Mission Conference in Montreat, North Carolina recently brought back the painful story of a visit to Zaire.

In the spring of 1970, I was flying from Lagos to Kinshasa on a big plane with only three passengers. Upon arrival the other two sailed through customs on familiar territory while I was held up for a body search (the first time that had happened to me). Then I was asked to pay an entrance fee of eighty dollars, which averaged out at twenty dollars a day for the four days I was scheduled to be there—a substantial part of my travel budget in those days. I had not been told about this fee in previous correspondence, and I did not want to pay it because of the dent it would make in my supply of traveler's checks.

I kept thinking that Don Bobb or someone else would come at any moment to rescue me, but no one did. As far as I knew, I had no reservations for lodging, and I definitely knew I had no telephone numbers. As darkness came, I felt some desperation. Then a bus showed up, and when I was asked my destination, I replied, "The American Embassy." In all the traveling I had done over the previous twenty-five years, I had never contacted an American Embassy!

The ride into the city of Kinshasa was one of the wildest I have ever known. The bus careened around breathtaking curves and finally hit a flagpole as we turned into the embassy grounds. As I climbed down from the bus, a car roared up from behind and a young man emerged and rushed toward me. "Could you be Margaret Flory?" he asked breathlessly.

"Yes, I could," I said with an uncustomary edge in my voice. He then introduced himself as the travel agency representative who was supposed to have met me at the airport! The great irony of it was that he carried in his pocket the letter from the general secretary of the Council of Churches of Zaire that would have saved me eighty dollars. This young man from the agency then took me to the Mission Guest House. Not a soul was to be seen (I later learned they were all at a high school musical), and so he showed me to my cabin. Just before leaving, he remembered that he had a note for me from Don Bobb.

The note, which I read later, said that Don was sorry not to be at the plane to meet me, but at the moment of my arrival he would be playing the piano for a high school musical directed by his wife. He invited me to come, and then join the young people for a pool party at his home later on.

By then the heat had gotten to me, and I was exhausted. But I knew that a shower and fresh clothes would keep me going, so I prepared to join the party. Remembering that I had seen a public telephone on the veranda of the compound office, I thought that perhaps I could summon a taxi, as I seemed to be all alone on the compound. Venturing forth in the dark, I stumbled and fell on a pile of rocks. As soon as I regained my footing, I fell again into a shallow hole along my path.

Then I remembered that it was Friday the thirteenth of May—my birthday! I decided it was not my special day after all. So I carefully groped my way back to the cabin where I had left a light burning. I was too agitated to sleep so I opened my briefcase and worked for three hours, preparing several packets of mail for the office back in New York.

When I looked out the window the next morning, I realized I was in the midst of a construction project. All around there were piles of rocks and holes in the ground, which fully explained my experience of the night before.

To add insult to injury, I learned that the flight on which I was to be leaving for Zambia in three days had been canceled. This meant staying a whole week in a place that was not a present favorite. Of course, I used the time to meet people and learn about mission in Zaire. But there is one final irony to this story of a birthday I would like to forget. The mail on which I had worked so hard reached New York several weeks after I did. I had to face the realization that the work I thought I had set into motion still remained to be done!

BREAK NOT THE CIRCLE

One of the extra joys of attending meetings at the headquarters of the World Council of Churches in Geneva was the possibility of seeing one's friends when the official sessions were over. On a certain day in the fall of 1977, I was scheduled to have lunch with Doreen Potter, wife of Philip Potter who at that time was general secretary of the World Council. While waiting to be picked up at the front door of the Ecumenical Center, I wandered into the bookstore to browse. I found there a new collection of hymns entitled *Break Not the Circle*, with music by Doreen Potter and words by Fred Kaan. Leafing through the hymn book, I liked what I read and bought it immediately, realizing that our luncheon conversation would be stimulated by the purchase.

Over lunch, Doreen told me of the work and the joy that had gone into the new book. Afterwards, she drove me to the Potter home, went to the piano and began to play and sing the songs. She went through the book from beginning to end, while I sat beside her on the piano bench. A unique combination of her native Jamaican lilt in the music and new meanings in the words by Fred Kaan made the songs very appropriate for changing times. That same afternoon, I identified my favorites, which would be used in countless meetings in countless settings in the years ahead: "Let Us Talents and Tongues Employ," "Help Us Accept Each Other" and "God Has Set Us Free."

Before leaving Geneva, I shared a dream with Doreen: to hold a music workshop at the Conference Center in Stony Point, New York. This dream was fulfilled in 1978 with the help of Louise Palm, when a group of music lovers gathered at the Gilmor Sloane House to get acquainted with Doreen and to sing her music. Doreen was very excited at being invited on her own merit to make her own creative contribution, and not just as the wife of an ecumenical leader.

Some months later, some of us listened in sadness as Philip Potter, while addressing the Presbyterian Women's Assembly at Purdue University, told of his wife's impending surgery for cancer. In the following months, friends coming from Geneva brought word of Doreen's brave fight. In June of 1980, I was in Geneva again for a meeting of the WCC Task Force on Ecumenical Sharing of Resources. Philip was a speaker at one of the sessions and arranged for me to see Doreen briefly, despite her extreme weakness. I found her filled with gratitude that she had been able to finish her work for the new edition of *Cantate Domino,* and even with hope that she might go to a meeting in Britain the following week.

But when I said goodbye, I knew that I was seeing her for the last time. Ten days later, back in the States, I was in a worship session at the Presbyterian Synod of the Lakes and Prairies at Coe College, Iowa, when I was called to the phone. It was a long distance call with word of Doreen's death. Returning to the session, I realized that the hymn being sung was "Let Us Talents and Tongues Employ," with music by Doreen Potter and words by Fred Kaan.

> Lord, for today's encounters
> With all who are in need,
> Who hunger for acceptance,
> For righteousness and bread.
> We need new eyes for seeing,
> New hands for holding on;
> Renew us with your Spirit,
> Lord, free us, make us one!

As I slipped into my seat, I thought, what a wonderful, unexpected memorial, and I was deeply comforted that the singing of Doreen's vibrant music would continue *ad infinitum.*

The circle has not been broken.

NEVER TOO LATE

One day in May 1978, I received a note that the general director of the United Presbyterian Program Agency, Oscar McCloud, would like to see me at my earliest convenience. I had no idea how much my remaining days on the Presbyterian national staff would be changed by the words that were to be spoken between us.

Oscar said he had in mind a long-range effort at transforming the church's understanding of its mission—and he wanted me to undertake such an assignment. Steps that might have been dragging on the way to see the general director were dancing on the way back. What an assignment for the last two years of one's vocational life! I could hardly wait to get going!

The first steps involved setting up an office, organizing a planning committee, and preparing an interpretive effort to help regional bodies and local churches understand the focus of this "Education for Mission" venture and to decide how they wanted to fit into it.

Getting rid of nineteenth century attitudes was not going to be easy. It had been fourteen years since the "Mission on Six Continents" theme had been articulated in a world mission conference in Mexico City. The International Missionary Council had become a part of the World Council of Churches in 1961. Thus, the WCC conference in Mexico City in 1964 was really a continuation of this international approach to mission. But to most American denominations, we were still the "sending" churches. We were just beginning to think about learning *with* and receiving *from* the churches of the world.

The new Education for Mission program for Presbyterians had as its purpose "the animation of the Christian community that it might widen its interests and invest its strengths to meet the challenges facing it in the world."

In the next two and a half years, the United Presbyterian Church, as it was known then, was enlivened considerably as synods, presbyteries, local churches and conference centers sought ways to respond, either seeking funds to fulfill dreams, or realigning resources locally. Building on projects initiated earlier, such as Frontier Internships, the Bi-National Service community, and the Mission to the USA program, which was already bringing to this country Christian leaders from other nations, the new Education for Mission program got underway. Until my retirement in 1980, I shuttled between offices on the fourth and eleventh floors of the Interchurch Center. On the eleventh floor, I was still a part of the ongoing People in Mission unit of the Presbyterian Program Agency; on the fourth floor, I was coordinating this special EFM project. While I shuttled between floors, June Kushino, whose skills and faithfulness were just right for this assignment, staffed the EFM office, and Paula Steffen came from Brazil to serve as the international staff assistant. And all across the world church, persons of responsibility were consulted on ways to aid congregations in seeking fresh ways of thinking globally and acting locally.

In its last year, the EFM project concentrated on holding eight conferences coast to coast, including one in Puerto Rico. Colleagues from overseas churches joined representatives of churches in the United States. The first series of conferences were held in Stony Point, Seattle, and Kansas City in April and May 1980. In June and July we held conferences in Aquadilla, Puerto Rico; Montreat, North Carolina; Muskingum, Ohio and Ghost Ranch, New Mexico.

Wherever the leaders went in team formation, they spoke passionately about the world's agenda where they lived, they told how people were hurting in their societies, and they suggested how the churches together should respond.

To depict the liveliness of this animating force, which was engaging hundreds of Presbyterians in reflection and dialogue toward action, Usha Barkat, a Pakistani artist, created four large mobiles composed of stick figures in black, red, white and yellow—representing the whole of humanity and bearing in several languages the words, "Celebrate Christ's Lively Community." There they were in all the conferences floating above the assembled conferees. In Aquadilla, where we were meeting out of doors, a sea breeze sat the mobile figures in motion. They were dancing in the wind in various formations, giving the impression of lively interaction, symbolic of the hope that seemed so appropriate for such a project.

Thus was fulfilled my dance down the hall years earlier following a conference with Oscar McCloud.

THE 1980S

THE AGE TO RESTYLE

RETURNING TO BERKELEY

My first post-retirement assignment in 1981 was at the Pacific School of Religion in Berkeley, California, where I was to serve as Minister in Residence. This entitled me to an apartment on the campus, a meal ticket in the refectory and an opportunity to audit any class I wanted. I had been there only a few days when I learned that Mark Jurgensmeyer of the University of California faculty would be giving a two-hour lecture in a classroom nearby. Some sixteen years earlier, Mark had served in India as a Frontier Intern, and I thought it would be fun to slip into class unnoticed and watch him in action. Sitting behind a very tall, broad-shouldered male, I thought I could be incognito. Knowing that Mark had already written a book on Gandhi and was brilliant in his field of comparative religion, I reflected on the value of overseas experience as an agent of transformation.

I remembered a reference to him in *New World Outlook* (at the time a joint Presbyterian/Methodist publication) as the "sitar playing missionary." I remembered his first message to me upon his return from India: "Dear Margaret: How can I do my own thing if I don't have my own things? In other words, where's my trunk?"

The trunk was located, but what did "Do my own thing" mean? I was to hear this phrase countless times in the coming days, and eventually I sensed its meaning. Constantly learning both the trivial and the sublime from the young as they move from one generation into the next has been my trademark! Constantly rejoicing in their spiritual growth and societal contributions has been my blessing.

All of a sudden, my attention was drawn from reverie and focused by the comment, "And now, before the class takes a break between sessions, I want you to meet my mentor, Miss Margaret Flory from New York."

There followed one of the most meaningful introductions I have ever had, accompanied by a big *abrazo* as the intermission began.

Suspense in Bangkok

Two missionary friends, Sally Wylie and Jean Bellerjeau, and a Thai friend, Boon Me Junkeree, were with me in the Bangkok airport on a January day in 1985 as I stood by a wagonful of luggage. I was understandably nervous because the cart contained more luggage than I had checked for boarding when I left the United States. A few days earlier in Hong Kong, during a consultation of the presidents of the Asian women's Christian colleges, I had received gifts from the ten colleges involved in the Asian Women's Institute (AWI).*

---

* The Asian Women's Institute came into being in 1975 when the presidents of the Asian Christian colleges for women, particularly those that had received assistance for their students through Church Women United's World Day of Prayer offerings, decided to form an umbrella institute to support one another and to find ways of working together for the education and advancement of Asian women.

Some of the gifts had been hastily packed at the end of the meeting in Hong Kong for shipment back to the United States, but many were still with me, including a rug from Kinnaird College in Pakistan.

When I checked in for a flight to New Delhi, I realized that I was in trouble as a consultation began behind the counter about the payment of overweight. Several Thai airline personnel were involved in the discussion, and I was kept waiting while others were checked through for the flight.

Somehow, I had left Hong Kong without paying overweight. Now I might have to hand over my total supply of traveler's checks to pay for the generosity extended by Asian friends in gratitude for my ten years of service with AWI.

Eventually, a smiling gentleman beckoned me back to the counter. My ticket and boarding pass were handed over with a kindly admonition, "Have a good flight, Miss Flory."

As my mood of discouragement gave way to relief, I found out what had really happened to change the dynamics behind the counter. Unseen by me, my Thai friend had managed to have a word with one of the persons in charge of tickets and luggage. She had said something like this: "Miss Flory is a great friend of Thailand. She has helped many of us doctors, nurses, teachers and pastors when we studied in the United States. We do not want her to be embarrassed, and we do not want to be embarrassed."

The luggage rolled away for loading, and after a quick hug all around, I boarded the plane to discover that not only had they overlooked the excess baggage, but they also had put me in the club class, which meant a wider seat, and had provided me with a travel kit and free drinks, which I did not need. As I settled into my seat, I was filled with recollections of many Thai young people whose destinies in the United States twenty years earlier had been handled from the Presbyterian Student World Relations desk. As Dietrich Bonhoeffer wrote, "Gratitude is the force that constantly rekindles memory." This time gratitude had gone full circle and won the day.

Mistaken Identity

Although I never knew Margaret Mead as a personal friend or a colleague, her name ran like a thread through my life. I remember Margaret Shannon's older sister, Winifred, coming to our apartment in New York from a conference on euthenics at Vassar College in the 1940s. She spoke with enthusiasm about the presence of a Margaret Mead, then a young anthropologist just back from her first field assignment in the South Pacific. Over the years, whenever I came across her writings in journals or her opinions on television, I found myself responding positively to her wisdom and inspiration.

Her book, *Culture and Commitment*, with its introduction of the "cluster approach,"* contained special insights that I applied in my "New Dimensions in Mission" efforts. I avidly read her autobiography, *Blackberry Winter*, enjoying the climate of her life as a graduate student at Columbia University on Morningside Heights, since it was a milieu also well known to me.

I was delighted to find that Ruth Benedict—whose famous book, *The Chrysanthemum and the Sword*, I had read before going to Japan in 1948—was Margaret Mead's mentor and close friend. It was the book my Japanese friends wanted most to borrow during my residence at Joshi Dai that year. They found it almost unbelievable that Miss Benedict, writing this book during World War II, had never been in Japan, and they simply could not understand how she could analyze their culture so effectively, never having set foot on their soil.

When Margaret Mead became involved in the Church and Society Division of the World Council of Churches I realized she was a staunch Episcopalian. Two of my friends, Paul Abrecht and Metropolitan Paulus Gregorious, quoted her often and described the impact of her presence at World

---

* Informal groupings of persons with common interests, concerns or goals.

Council of Churches events. I myself was present at the Uppsala, Sweden assembly in 1968 where her presence was heralded by the media. I particularly remember her creative contribution in an after-hours coffeehouse atmosphere there, when she bonded with the young people and joined their lively conversations. She liked to say, "For the first time, the young are seeing history being made before it is censored by their parents."

Some four years later, I made the acquaintance of Margaret Mead's daughter, Catherine Bateson, who came to Memphis, Tennessee for a special seminar on education for women, which brought together a group of women educators from Asia and the Middle East.

By that time, Catherine Bateson was teaching at Damavand College in Teheran, Iran. A few months later, I organized a travel-study seminar of women educators to the Middle East, and the principal lecturer for our time in Teheran was Catherine Bateson.

In 1978, in the midst of an event sponsored by the Asian Women's Institute in Korea, a young woman leaned across the table to query, "Are you Margaret Mead?" I surprised myself with my answer: "No, but I would rather think like her than look like her."

Ten years later in a midtown restaurant in New York City, the waitress who brought my check asked, "Did anyone ever tell you how much you look like Margaret Mead?" This time I was left with no rejoinder.

Toward the end of her life, Margaret Mead preached an unforgettable sermon in an Episcopal church in Connecticut, a sermon that was later excerpted in the Church Women United publication called *The Church Woman*. In this sermon, she articulated ideas that I have used over and over in articles and speeches related to global education for mission.

"We are faced with a world in which we need to defend something more than the ground beneath our feet," she observed. "Defending the little bit of space on which one stands, sits, plants a tree or builds a church is no longer the basic problem.

"Now it is the question of shared atmosphere and shared oceans that cannot be protected, where no gun can drive away the accumulated contamination that may destroy both the ocean and the air. What people do in one part of the world endangers the whole."

Then she asked the key question: "How are we going to combine people's dedication to community and country so that they will work hard enough to protect the atmosphere and the oceans, and yet not go to war over the lines of national sovereignty, as they have in the past? I think this will happen only if, when you join a larger group, you do not betray the smaller one . . . When our fathers and mothers, our friends and the members of our own group are within the whole of humankind, then the world is no longer a mass or an enemy, but a part of one's self."

Yes, I have learned a lot from Margaret Mead. As was true for her, life and work have been closely interwoven for me also. Both of us loved young people, and, like Margaret Mead, I have had a tendency to press forward to where the future was breaking into the present and the past. Both of us were intensely interested in the peoples of the whole wide world. Where the world was her classroom, it has been my parish.

But unlike Margaret Mead, who had three husbands, I have had none; and whereas she traveled with a staff of wood, I usually traveled with too much luggage.

NEW EYES FOR SEEING

"Miss Flory, do you realize that you could be declared legally blind?" This startling question from Dr. Eleanor Faye, eminent New York specialist in limited vision, provided the push that transformed my life. My answer, "But can anything be done about it?" brought the response, "I can operate."

For as long as I can remember, I had experienced eye trouble—a combination, so they said, of nearsightedness and astigmatism. Over and over again, doctors fitted me with new glasses that I did not wear because they did not help my eyesight.

The time came when I could no longer read the arrival and departure signs at the airports, nor could I read signs at street corners from a bus or a car. I too often could no longer sing in church because I could not read the hymns. (Fortunately, many were in my memory bank.) I did not see steps nor side railings, and took many a fall. Dr. Faye's words, "I'm going to make you less nearsighted," brought new hope.

At the hospital, there was an unnerving setback when the anesthesiologist refused to assist in the operation because of the results of a last-minute cardiogram. So I was sent home to wear a heart monitor for two weeks and visit a cardiac center for prescribed stress tests. Finally, I was cleared with the comment, "You may always have had extra heartbeats!"

After the operation, when Dr. Faye removed the bandages, I was overwhelmed with joy at the new sight in my left eye. My heart soared as I prepared to leave the hospital, taking care not to bend or lift. When I was finally ready, I sat down on a chair to wait for Louise Palm of Stony Point, who was coming to take me home. As I waited, I began to test the new eye, saying aloud in amazement, "It is a *miracle*—it is a *miracle*!" Then it happened. The young woman who had come unnoticed to clean the room began to sing a song in her soft African American gospel rhythm that went something like this:

It took a miracle to put the world in place;
It took a miracle to hang the stars;
And when he saved my soul, and made me whole,
It was a miracle of peace and love.

By the time she finished singing it twice, I felt a Divine Presence within the room, sending me out with new eyes for seeing—new eyes that were filled with tears of gratitude.

SALUTING PIONEERS IN GUATEMALA

In 1987 I was asked to be staff-at-large for the celebration of 150 years of "Presbyterian Witness in the World." As I was working on program ideas and resources for the denomination-wide celebration, it occurred to me to experiment with a program idea at the Gilmor Sloane House at Stony Point.

Harkening back to my early training at Ohio University and my interest in dramatic interpretation, I decided to choose four women missionaries whose work was unique and whom I knew personally or through their writings. One of the four was Dorothy Peck.* This took me back to 1946 when I had my first look at the world beyond my own country.

As organizer of a traveling seminar for business and professional women, I accompanied sixteen women and one man to Guatemala. It was Christmas time and we were to be gone three weeks. It may have been the very first travel and study venture abroad sponsored by a national church for lay people who paid their own way. Even after almost fifty years there are so many vivid memories: the scenic beauty of Lakes Atitlan and Amatitlan, the volcanoes, our first glimpse of bougainvillea in many luscious shades, poinsettia branches covering the white-washed walls of little churches, the marimba music that set our feet dancing, the spectacular religious processions, the *nascimientos* (Christmas creches) in every home, the sheer precipices on the roads where there were no guard rails, Christmas carols in other languages, the children wide-eyed at the sight of so many North American women wearing hats, the rich colors and variety of Indian dress, the many burdens carried on the head or back. We did not fail to notice the poverty and the pain, but neither could we fail to see this land of eternal spring through rose-colored glasses.

* The other three were Dr. Dorothy Foster of the Ferozepur Hospital on the border of India and Pakistan; Helen Reischauer, missionary in Japan who founded the deaf oral school, Rowa Gakko; and Jean Kenyon MacKenzie who immortalized Cameroonian Christian life with her writings.

On a visit to the Mam Christian Center I had my first glimpse of a pioneering missionary effort, which, in retrospect, seems unique in all the world. The directors of the Mam Center, Dorothy and Dudley Peck, went to Guatemala as Presbyterian missionaries with degrees from Princeton Seminary and Wellesley College. They had told the mission board they wanted to work with indigenous peoples. Their location was at Quezaltenango in the mountains of Guatemala where we spent Christmas week, attending services, meeting the witch doctor whose conversion to Christianity had helped their work, singing from hymnals they had created, hearing the Gospel of Jesus Christ in the Mam language, watching Dorothy Peck preaching in the market, attired like the Indian women all around her.

What I found incredible then, and still do, was the fact that the Mam language had never been written down until the Pecks began to write it as they heard it from the lips of the Mam people. What could be more elemental and creative than mastering a native language and writing it down? In this task, the Pecks had the help of the linguistic laboratory at the University of Chicago. Teams of linguists came from the university summer after summer to help with the gigantic task of recording the language so that the scriptures could be translated, giving the people the gospel in their own language.

In preparation for the presentation involving Dorothy Peck, I contacted the Peck's daughter in Atlanta, who expressed great interest in my plan and offered to send materials, including a copy of the hymnbook in the Mam language that her mother had prepared. Before our conversation was over, she said, "There is one story about mother that we children like best of all." Then she told me that one day when her mother was preaching in the marketplace with a basket of literature in the Mam language by her side, the peaceful scene was disturbed by some young troublemakers. They crept up behind her and set her skirts on fire! Instead of crying out or giving in to panic, she beat the flames out with her hands, backed herself against a wall for protection, and finished her sermon! Both her skirt and her heart were on fire that day.

In later years, when I looked back, I remembered the work of the Pecks as one of the most meaningful missions I had ever seen. I remembered the privilege I had experienced of being with the Guatemalan Indians when dignity had not been taken away and they did not live in daily fear. Over the years, I watched in agony the brutalization of the Guatemalan people, the tyrannies, the sadness, the total violation of their human rights.

Sharing the experience has undoubtedly been stimulated by the arrival of several Guatemalans in my presbytery, Western North Carolina, which now has a partnership with the Presbyterian Church of Guatemala. Their presence has reminded me that the context for the missionary relationship has changed completely in fifty years but the gospel message remains the same. And so, my mind rehearsed the whole cycle: the coming of missionaries, the mastering of the language, the translation of the scriptures, the organizing of the churches for worship, preaching, and education, and finally the development of international partnerships in mission and the emerging of a worldwide Christian community.

Thus, in writing about the Pecks' work among the Mam peoples in Guatemala, I also want to pay tribute to all pioneering missionaries who launched into the unknown, guided by God's Spirit, to help lay the foundation for the church universal.

THE 1990S

------- ❖ -------

TIME TO REMEMBER

FAREWELL TO MORNINGSIDE HEIGHTS

During my last days before leaving New York for North Carolina—after fifty years of living in New York City—I was going through the "last time" syndrome. One afternoon, as I walked by the new entrance to Union Seminary at Broadway and 121st Street in Manhattan, I looked through to the quadrangle and remembered fifty years earlier when I had made an entrance into the world of seminary and church.

The summer of 1940 was a watershed summer. I was leaving the world of teaching and preparing to enter campus ministry that fall at my alma mater, Ohio University, as director of the Presbyterian Westminster Foundation. Looking back on that summer I remember:

> The ability of Dr. Harry Emerson Fosdick to enthrall the summer congregation at the Riverside Church, with its large number of students from Columbia University. Hearing him meant going very early to one of two packed services on Sunday morning.

The Commons at Union Seminary in the 1940s when concern for the intermingling of politics and faith was accented at every gathering—by students from the whole world.

The back-and-forth pacing of Professor Reinhold Niebuhr as he thundered prophetically in the summer lecture series.

"The best teacher of them all." That was the way I summed up Dr. Mary Ely Lyman of Union, whose New Testament course on the life and teachings of Jesus was a milestone of my student days.

The pigeons. In those days, they added a romantic touch in the courtyards of New York, but after struggling with them over the years at Morningside Gardens where they made a nest on my balcony, I have lost my affection for pigeons.

Joining other Ohioans for conversation and snacks under the buckeye tree on the Columbia University campus. Now, the state trees are gone and in their stead are the stone and steel of new buildings.

The glowing sunsets over New Jersey as seen from Morningside Heights. I felt a little sad that after fifty years only the sunsets remained the same.

Better Late Than Without Shoes

Shoes, shoes, shoes—they have been the bane of my life.

In my youth, my shoe size was so large that I had trouble finding shoes to fit. When I started traveling far and wide in connection with my work among the world's students, I took either too many shoes, resulting in luggage overweight, or too few shoes, which brought the embarrassment of mismatched colors. Light in a New York apartment closet, sometimes dim, resulted in combinations such as one black and one navy blue shoe. Shoes were sometimes left in closets or under beds, causing trouble for the exasperated hostess or the weary lost-and-found stations of many a hotel or pension.

But the following moment was perhaps the most embarrassing of all. I was on my way to Paris in September 1990 for the General Assembly of the World Student Christian Federation. I had been in my new home in Brevard, North Carolina for only six days, and the boxes were piled high in every room. I was exhausted from the move from a nine-closet New York apartment to a three-closet apartment in Brevard.

Why am I doing this, I asked my weary self on the Air France plane. I had retired as president of the WSCF Trustees in the U.S. but my successor was committed to another assignment and urged me to go. For me, the discipline of saying yes to a new idea or a new assignment has always been stronger than the discipline of saying no. This has got to change with advancing age, I told myself. Then I kicked off my shoes and fell asleep.

When I awoke, it was light and we were approaching Paris. There was the usual scurry before arrival and I was a major player as I searched for my shoes, first under my seat and then around surrounding seats. No shoes in sight! I went up and down the aisles, looking to the left and to the right, lamely explaining my predicament to the curious. One glance at my feet should have told the story. Finally I returned to my seat and rang for the flight attendant. She seemed sympathetic and said she would try to find them.

The plane landed, taxied to the gate, and emptied all of its passengers but one, who could not face walking out shoeless to greet a young emissary of the WSCF. In the meantime, the flight attendant and three helpers were frantically but methodically searching the plane, wading in the debris of the departed. Finally a cry, "Here they are!"

The shoes were in the middle section at the back of the plane, where they probably had been kicked by successive passengers in the night. The relief of the flight attendant was almost as great as mine as I muttered to myself, "Was this trip necessary?" and hurried off to meet the French student still waiting at the gate with his WSCF "Welcome" placard.

THE GIFT OF AN OPEN DOOR

Dr. Edwin Espy, retired general secretary of the National Council of Churches, died in 1993. In my imagination, from my home in Brevard, North Carolina, I joined with others who had gathered at the Interchurch Center in New York for a memorial service soon after his death.

I recalled one moment forty years earlier, when one sentence uttered by Ed Espy changed my whole life. I don't remember much else about the executive committee meeting of the SVM (Student Volunteer Movement), but I do remember my utter disbelief when I heard Ed Espy, in a discussion about leadership for the planning committee of the next SVM quadrennial meeting, suggest the name of Margaret Flory. For a man, even in the campus ministry, to name a woman to head an important responsibility was indeed a rarity. I recall asking him to think the matter over and to consult with my superiors at the Presbyterian headquarters where I was employed. He did consult and the appointment came through.

That marked the beginning for me of a cycle of eight years of planning, organizing and following up on two large quadrennial student events at my alma mater, Ohio University. The first was the Ecumenical Student Conference on the Christian World Mission in 1955 with "Revolution and Reconciliation" as the theme. Students in attendance at that event represented ninety-eight countries. Then in 1959 I helped organize the North American Student Conference on "Frontiers," an event of "Inquiry and Involvement." Both of these were conferences of up to four thousand students with a goal of fifty percent coming from abroad.

Thank you, Ed Espy, for your ecumenical vision for Student Christian Movements, and for being ahead of your time in so many ways. Your role as a door-opener for me was crucial.

GIVING THANKS FOR FRIENDS

Every Thanksgiving Day I follow the practice of remembering, in gratitude, those persons who have meant the most to me in past years. On the list are two Asian women, no longer living, who entered my life in 1946: the Rev. Tamaki Uemura and Dr. Josefa Ilano.

I have written earlier of a moment in time when, as a tiny girl I had said goodbye to my birth mother. In 1982, as a grown woman, I was to say goodbye to Tamaki Uemura, who had been as a mother to me for more than thirty years. While in Hong Kong with a China Seminar, I received a cable summoning me to Japan. Tamaki was in a coma when I arrived at her bedside. I knelt and poured out the feelings of my heart. There was no change of expression on her serene face, but my hands felt movement in her body, and I sensed she knew that Masuko-san, her adopted daughter, was there. She died the next day, leaving me with a host of memories.

As I have observed in previous stories, soon after the end of World War II, Christians from nations that had fought against one another during the war began to seek ways to break down the barriers between their countries and peoples. Both Tamaki Uemura and Josefa Ilano were a part of an East Asia Fellowship Mission visiting different parts of the United States speaking of the need for reconciliation.

When these travels were over, Dr. Ilano decided to stay longer in the United States to accept some of the invitations that had been extended to her. Learning that I was going to take a traveling seminar to Guatemala for three weeks at Christmas, she wanted to go along at her own expense. With her cheerful spirit, her facility in the Spanish language and her Filipina dresses with the butterfly sleeves, she made a unique contribution to the life of the traveling seminar.

The blessing of her presence during the 1946 Christmas season in Guatemala brought an insight that stayed with me. In years to come, as I sent groups out or traveled with them, I always found a way for the travel groups to be international. I discovered that when persons of different cultures and nationalities are drawn together in a common experience, they teach each other in life-changing ways.

In the years to come, whenever I went to the Philippines, no matter who was hosting my visit, Dr. Ilano staged her own welcome party, composed of close Filipino friends—hers and mine. And always there were special gifts. Because Doctora, as they called her, had brought into the world the sons and daughters of most of my missionary friends in the Philippines, there was always a marvelous circle of people who gathered to celebrate. In her later years, she managed the Country Bake Shop on United Nations Avenue in Manila—a favorite breakfast and coffee spot for politicians and for all her friends.

At the same time, she continued her medical work through the World Health Organization. On one occasion, our paths crossed in London, a blessed surprise for both of us.

The great love of her life was Silliman University in Dumaguete, Philippines. This struck a responsive chord in my heart, for ever since my month's visit in 1948, Silliman by the Sea has been a very special place for me. Dr. Ilano was the first woman trustee of Silliman, serving on its board for twenty-seven years, and as chairperson for seventeen of those years.

When Dr. Ilano died in 1992, a memorial service was held at Silliman with a special tribute by the president, Angel Alcala. He said that she had enrolled at Silliman when it was known to be a school for boys, but that she was not one to be intimidated by gender. He referred to her as Silliman's "Grand Old Lady" who represented grace under pressure as she presided over an all-male board.

Tamaki Uemura preceded Josefa Ilano in death by ten years, but from 1946 to 1983, they kept in close touch with each other and with me.

On Thanksgiving Day in 1993, looking back in profound gratitude, I marveled at God's leading in that moment in time almost fifty years ago, when three lives from the Pacific and Atlantic worlds were linked in enduring friendship and creative interaction for the sake of harmony and community in God's world.

WATCHDOG

Once a year the seminary students from Yale, Union and Princeton came to 156 Fifth Avenue, the Presbyterian mission headquarters in New York City, for a briefing on mission and interchurch service. I was in charge of these briefings and always enjoyed having a look at the future leadership of the church.

During one such briefing sometime in the early 1950s, one of the speakers was Be Ruys, a Dutch woman who had been ordained for a specific postwar assignment: the directorship of the Hendrich Kraemer House in Berlin, a center that had recently opened for Dutch-speaking persons in postwar Berlin and was named for the eminent Dutch theologian, Dr. Hendrick Kraemer.

Be was talking about the wartime role of Christians caught in the Nazi crisis. She was reaching for a word she could not find in her English vocabulary, and so she simply barked, "Bow wow! Bow wow!" At that moment a chorus went up from the seminarians: "Watchdog," they cried, "Watchdog!" In relief she clapped her hands and cried, "Yes, watchdog on the wall," referring to the image of the watchman on the wall in biblical literature, whose task it was to warn of approaching danger. This exchange delighted the seminarians and they joined in the clapping.

This incident came to mind recently when I was reading Mary Glazener's stirring novel based on the life of Dietrich Bonhoeffer, *The Cup of Wrath.* The book reveals with startling clarity the way the members of the Confessing Church of Germany took their stand as watchdogs against a mounting Nazi tyranny.

In the passage that catapulted my memory back to Be Ruys and the seminarians, Dietrich Bonhoeffer is speaking to a relative, voicing his oneness with the Barmen Declaration of the Confessing Church* and expressing his concern for the steadfastness of the church in the face of persecution. His message was this: "The church must stand as a watchman and speak to the need of the times, no matter what it costs."

Be Ruys carried on her amazing ministry into the 1990s. Recently she retired from the directorship of Hendrick Kraemer House. All those years she ministered to the Dutch Christians in Berlin, probed the key issues of life and faith with every student generation, kept in touch as a reconciler with the Christians in East Germany, and published regularly information on the churches of the two Germanys for the wider ecumenical community. I was one of her friends and admirers who kept in touch with issues and people through Be, one of the most effective networkers of all! Always she has been one of those watchdogs—a sentinel for peace and justice for our times.

---

* The Confessional Synod of the German Evangelical Church met in Barmen, May 29–31, 1934. Here representatives from all the German Confessional Churches agreed upon what has come to be known as "The Barmen Confession." Warning against the rising influence of Nazism on the church in Germany, they proclaimed: "We publicly declare before all evangelical churches in Germany that what they hold in common in this confession is grievously imperiled . . . "

RIGHT PEOPLE, RIGHT PLACE, RIGHT TIME

On a certain evening in 1972, Jim and Louise Palm, in Hong Kong for a few days, joined me for dinner at a restaurant on the Peak, where guests ascend by cable tram to see the glorious vistas of Hong Kong surrounding the restaurant in all directions. I was in Hong Kong for an evaluation/planning event related to the Frontier Internship program in Asia. They were visiting from the Philippines, where Jim was a Protestant chaplain at the University and Louise was working with several music programs in the area.

I remember talking to them about the Stony Point Center and asking if they would ever consider an assignment as directors of such a place, for which, it seemed to me, they were perfectly equipped. They said that they wanted to stay where they were as long as there was a creative place for them there. Unless they needed to return home for family reasons such as children's education or the health of their parents, they planned to stay. This conversation, however, proved useful for the future.

The scene shifts to the spring of 1973. The United Presbyterian Church is being restructured at the national and regional levels. The members of the staff of the Commission on Ecumenical Mission and Relations (COEMAR) in which I held a wonderful post entitled "New Dimensions in Mission," were asked to resign to allow a new structure to emerge. One day, in a church guest house in Yaoundé, Cameroon, I sat in my room in reflection, looking out at a distant horizon and pondering my future. I was fifty-nine years old, too young to retire, and—it seemed to me then—too old to start a new profession. It was a very low moment in my life, and I prayed earnestly for guidance. Somehow, out of that morning of prayer and reflection, came the strong conviction that my future was related to the Gilmor Sloane House at Stony Point with which I had been closely affiliated since 1949 when this marvelous old victorian home had come to the church from the four Gilmor sisters, as a gift for missionary purposes.

By 1973, the Stony Point Missionary Orientation Center had been closed and the only action on the Center grounds was at the Gilmor Sloane House, which would probably be a base for whatever happened next. And so I returned from Africa, feeling that my destiny lay in some way with this very special place, but I told no one and waited for life to move forward.

In due time, I was offered the position of Associate for Human Resource Planning in the newly designed Program Agency of the United Presbyterian Church, USA, and, almost overnight, we were all caught up in making the new structure work.

The operation at Stony Point limped along with interim staff at the Gilmor Sloane House until 1975 when the Palm family returned from the Philippines and undertook what I called "The Stony Point Challenge."

The big break came when the national church decided to sell the missionary apartment complex at 47 Claremont Avenue, next to the Interchurch Center, in order to buy back from the other cooperating denominations their shares of what had been the MOC (Missionary Orientation Center) at Stony Point. The new Stony Point Center opened its doors in April 1977, offering a marvelous opportunity for the combined gifts of Jim and Louise Palm in building a base for global education in mission. Their personalities, charm and natural leadership, along with their integrity and Christian commitment were a "golden fit." They described the Center as "the place where the world becomes an open house." In addition to the surrounding churches using it as a place for spiritual retreat and advance, an ethos was developed in the complex of buildings and grounds by the highlighting and upholding of one justice cause after another, all the time planning for the annual coming of people from all over the world for "Global Village" experiences.

From my own post at the Interchurch Center where I was developing patterns of ecumenical sharing and programs of Education for Mission, I began working closely with Jim and Louise on a variety of projects. Then, one October day in 1980 when retirement loomed on the horizon for me, they appeared together in my office with the startling comment, "Everyone thinks that you should come to Stony Point with the Gilmor Sloane House as your base." It had been eight years since the vision in Cameroon. In the words of Han Suyin, in her novel, *The Mortal Flower,* "Time watched, crouched in its corner, the future was being prepared..." Although the invitation was not anticipated, I knew at once that the ultimate answer had to be, "Yes, if you can wait till I can fulfill a few other commitments."

And so it was that I spent the years between 1981 and 1988 at the Gilmor Sloane House, first supervising the new decorations and then serving as the program director. Members of the world Christian family kept coming to Stony Point for special projects. It was a perfect place for meetings of Bi-National Servants, for newly appointed missionaries and volunteers, for overseas and mission advocates serving in the presbyteries. Somewhere on the grounds, there would usually be international resource persons for any conceivable subject. It truly was "a place where the world becomes an open house."

In this sketch, I have encapsulated twenty-two years, highlighting a moment in Hong Kong, in Yaoundé, in New York, and finally in Stony Point. Now, back in Stony Point on this morning of January 4, 1994, I am reflecting on last night's glorious occasion when a host of friends and colleagues gathered to express gratitude to two who will always be remembered as "the right people, in the right place, at the right time"—Jim and Louise Palm.

Postscript

In telling the stories that have filled this book, certain strategic moments in time have been omitted, perhaps because I felt they related more to my personal magic moments than to the church vocation that propelled this undertaking. Yet, precisely because they were crucial moments for me, often influencing the future in ways I understand better by looking back than I could have understood at the time, I now feel some mention should be made of them.

In 1980, out of the blue, came a great weekend of celebration sponsored by the "Friends of Margaret Flory"—a retirement dinner attended by several hundred people at the Riverside Church in New York, followed by an all-day forum at Stony Point, highlighting the various themes of my vocational years. It fulfilled a cherished dream of having all my dear family, friends and colleagues in one room at the same time.

It also opened for me a floodgate of memories. I recalled life-shaping events that went all the way back to high school days. In 1931, as a high school junior, I was recognized by the governor of Ohio for placing first in a competitive examination in American history given at Bowling Green State University. This may have been a signal to me that hard work and serious study pay off.

Being selected for Phi Beta Kappa in my junior year of college, and then in my senior year winning the Ohio championship in intercollegiate debate with two other colleagues, and graduating magna cum laude from Ohio University, may have been additional signposts of the value placed in living up to one's abilities.

But I also recall that when I passed into the work-a-day world, first in education, and then in the church, no one seemed to pay much attention to academic records. The important questions were, did I love the people with whom I was working, and did I serve them with heart and mind, soul and strength?

Early on, I seemed to have learned to listen carefully to the other person and then to try to do something positive about the concern I had heard. In working with young people, as I did for twenty-five years, it was important to remain in the background, putting forth ideas when appropriate, never expecting to get the credit if those ideas took wings. Yet, midway through those years, there was the Alumni Certificate of Merit to let me know that I was still remembered at Ohio University.

Since my retirement celebration, meaningful citations have continued, such as those from the Korean Scholars Association, Silliman University in the Philippines, Zeta Tau Alpha, and the Asian Women's Institute. Surprises in my autumn years, such as the Women of Faith award from Presbyterian Women and an honorary doctorate in Humane Letters from Maryville College in Tennessee helped to reinforce my confidence that the Holy Spirit reveals and leads, opening new challenges and possibilities until the very end.

But the biggest surprise of all, coming on September 25, 1993, when I thought there could be no more on the horizon, was the naming of a building in Geneva, Switzerland, "The Margaret Flory Conference Hall" on the occasion of the fortieth anniversary celebration of the John Knox International Reformed Center.

Yet nothing in life can match the blessings that have come with the empowerment of so many younger friends who are making unique contributions in their own way and who keep me in touch with the present as it makes its way into the future.

T. S. Eliot may have expressed precisely the twin axioms of my life in a scene from *The Cocktail Party* when Edward says, "Oh, it isn't much that I understand yet, but Sir Henry has been saying, I think, that every moment is a fresh beginning, and Julia, that life is only keeping on. And somehow, the two ideas seem to fit together."

And so it is with me . . . working, loving, praying—still fresh beginnings, still keeping on.